TABLE OF CONTENTS

United States - Treasury Silver Lifesaving Medal

INTRODUCTION

The success of **VERNON'S COLLECTORS' GUIDE TO ORDERS, MEDALS AND DECORATIONS,** in all three editions, indicated to me that there was a need for an up to date work on collecting that goes into much more detail than the above, would serve the beginning collector in particular with much needed basic information and would also help the more advanced collector advance even further.

Thus, this book is dedicated to the proposition that all collectors are not created equal, but that they can become so with the acquisition of knowledge. There is much information "out there" that can benefit the collector, but it is scattered in so many places. The aim is to bring as much of this information together as is practicable and useful. The emphasis is on the United States, Great Britain and Germany because that is where there is the greatest interest in collecting.

Nevertheless, there will be general information that will apply to many countries, with the accent being on the avoidance of pitfalls. The extensive bibliography is not only to point out references I may have used, but also to provide to the reader sources for more information.

The central objective is to provide a reference that will give more information on the medals themselves, as opposed to their particular worth. The stress is on identification by providing information on details on the awards, such as symbols, inscriptions, dates, and naming or numbering where appropriate. I hope that this book will be regarded as a companion volume to the aforementioned VERNON'S COLLECTORS' GUIDE.

Obviously, not all items one comes across present a problem in identification. So, what has been done is to cover those items that seem to present some difficulty. Remember, if you are a specialist in a particular country then the problems of identification won't exist. The purpose of the book is to expand your horizons.

The collector has several avenues to approach the hobby:

1. The area of collecting. This is a matter which should be taken very seriously. Collecting the whole world can be fun at first, but ultimately very confusing. So having a focus for your collecting is of prime importance.

2. Identification. Being able to identify the items you collect is also of importance. Here is where the collector has to make a choice of buying reference books. I believe that there is no such thing as an "expensive book", only expensive mistakes that you incur by not buying them. Being able to identify the things you collect is central to the enjoyment of your hobby. This work is designed specifically to help you identify by a variety of methods the Orders, Medals, and Decorations that will pass through your hands.

3. Historical information. Why the medals etc came to be, and what they represent also is of considerable consequence to your collecting.

4. Numismatic information. The metal they were struck from, size, and numbers awarded are all pertinent.

5. Research possibilities. The collectors of British awards, and to a somewhat lesser extent American awards, have the ability to research the recipient of their items. This can greatly enhance, and personalize the course, and cause of collecting.

Acknowledgments:

A number of people have assisted me in the development of this book. I want to thank Roger Salisch who first gave me the idea for it, and assisted me to further its aims. Once again I am very fortunate to have the help and expertise of my good friend, Adam Rohloff, who besides dealing with all matters technical, played an important part in crystallizing my thoughts on several occasions. Moreover, he advanced me into the modern world by proposing that I work in Word Perfect 6.1. His role in this work cannot be underestimated. Amy Vernon's editing cleaned up much of my verbal Niagara. My thanks also to J. Robert Elliott who graciously gave me access to items in his collection for photographing. My discussions with collectors while this was an ongoing project also aided me immeasurably.

The love and support of my daughters Amy and Elizabeth Vernon; and Elizabeth's husband Hassan, and other family members, friends all made a contribution to my well-being which brought this work to fruition.

Notwithstanding any assistance all errors are the author's.

Editorial Assistant; Technical Advisor; Photography
Adam G. Rohloff

Style Editor:
Amy Vernon

Technical Consultants:
Elizabeth Vernon, Hassan Mneimneh

Sources of Photographed Material:
J. Robert Elliott, Adam G. Rohloff, Sydney B. Vernon

GENERAL CONCEPTS

Some of the material found in this section will be expanded in other places, including the Glossary, but it is always useful to have some basic understandings.

Metallic Composition

Orders, Medals, and Decorations are made from metal, with few exceptions. There are some plastic awards, but they need not be gone into here. The three basic metals are gold, silver, and bronze. Others have been used, such as platinum, copper; nickel, cupro-nickel, zinc, pewter, brass, and what has euphemistically been called "pot metal" or "war metal".

Further refinements include silver/gilt = goldplated or gold washed silver, giving items a "gold" or "golden" appearance. Thus, the term gold/gilt should never be used. There is also bronze/gilt = goldplated or goldwashed bronze, giving items a "gold" or "golden" look. Sometimes a base metal has been silver plated or washed to give a "silver" appearance. The item is then called "silvered".

At varying times, badges of Orders were usually gold and enameled. Gradually, for economic reasons the gold was changed to silver/gilt or bronze/gilt. Breast stars were almost always silver, sometimes gilded to indicate a special class. The insignia of most Orders were enameled, while most medals were not.

Many times, but not always, items are marked, as to metallic content. Any pieces marked 968, 958, 925, 900, 800 are, or should be, silver; referring to parts out of 1000. For example, 925 is the number for sterling silver. Conversely, any item marked sterling should be 925 silver. Some silver awards of the U.S.A. are marked sterling, as are some of the Philippines. Silver awards of France are often marked argent. Imperial German items may or may not be marked with a number, 800 and 900 being the most common. One German Medal, the Wuertemburg Merit Medal in Gold is marked 375, which equals 9 carat gold. The gold mark of Austrian Orders is usually 750, which equals 18 carat.

British gold and silver marks are to a standard established by the Goldsmiths and Silversmiths Guilds several centuries ago, and the system of punch marks indicating city, date and metal are firmly in place. Depending on the time period, British gold insignia may vary between 14 and 22 carat gold. Imperial Russian marks are on a different basis. The common Russian mark for silver is 84; 84 parts out of 96, slightly below sterling silver. The common gold mark is 56. This stands for 56 parts out of 96, roughly 14 carat gold.

7

Shapes of Awards

Many medals and decorations are circular, but some are oval. The cross in many styles is favored. Gallantry awards for many countries appear in cross style, others like the U.S.A. and Soviet Russia favored a star, namely, the Medals of Honor, and the Hero of the Soviet Union.

The breast stars of Orders have ranged from four to eight points, although some so-called stars are really like massive breast crosses similar to those of the Swedish Orders.

Widths of ribbons

The general width of ribbons depends on a basic principle, namely, the grade of the awards. The badge of the highest class of an Order, or the badge in a one class Order normally is worn hanging from a very wide ribbon called a sash. This ribbon is worn over one shoulder, across the chest. The next grade is normally worn at the neck on a ribbon described as a necklet, neck ribbon or a cravat. The lower grades are worn on a narrower ribbon on the breast. They may have a device of some kind on them to indicate class, or some special mention.

Naming of Awards

Some countries engage in the naming of their awards. This is particularly true in the case of Great Britain. Unnamed medals and decorations are the exceptions. Campaign medals are usually named around the rim, with the recipient's serial number, rank and unit, plus postnomial letters for any Orders or Decorations that have been won.

The German named awards include the Brunswick, and Hannover Waterloo Medals, as well as a few lifesaving medals. France and Belgium have issued some named lifesaving medals. Decorations of the United States of America have either been issued named, or some provision was made for naming. Two campaign medals, the West Indies Naval Campaign Medal (the Sampson Medal), and the Manila Bay Medal (the Dewey Medal) were officially named. One can also find some of the older campaign medals unofficially named. Good Conduct Medals of the various armed forces are frequently found named, especially the older issues. The various grades of the Italian Valor Medal can be found named also.

Documents Relating to Orders Medals, and Decorations

Most countries have the practice of issuing some type of document with their awards. They might be called diplomas, award certificates, or brevets. Some are very ornate with a facsimile of the award. Some may have sealing wax or seals impressed on the paper, or the earlier parchment documents. Some may have the signature of a famous person or monarch, thus having intrinsic value in their own right. Belgium for example, awards a document, and leaves it to the recipient to buy the actual decoration, etc. A document with a medal therefore may help in its identification.

Cases, Boxes, Containers of Award

The presentation of an Order, Medal, or Decoration can be done in a variety of ways. Sometimes they are presented by a high ranking official of the government or armed forces. There is usually some kind of container which can vary from a very elaborate lacquer case with strings and tassels, to a simple paper bag with the name of the award on it. Many U.S. items since World War II have come in a small blue cardboard box. Many awards of the Empire and Republics of Austria have come in a case with a rounded end. Some cases may be leather, cloth, wood or combination of materials. For a period from the late 19th century to World War I, Japanese medals came in balsa wood boxes. In the 1920's the country switched to fabric covered cardboard.

Some collectors feel that an award is incomplete without the original container. This is truer of the higher valued, or rarer items.

Condition of items

The condition of the items you collect has to be viewed on several levels. First, unless the item is rare, or very cheap, you should buy your material in the best possible condition, taking into account the nature and age of a piece. For example, some of the World War I European material is made of zinc or "war metal", not very good for long-term preservation. Therefore, trying to find a Troop Cross of Austria in pristine condition is not easy.

The collector can take several approaches in classifying condition. Since there is a carryover from coin collecting there is a tendency to use numismatic terms such as FDC (fleur de coin), mint or uncirculated for an item virtually in its original state. The next major category is EF, extra fine, indicating some minor wear; followed by VF, very fine, indicating some more serious wear, perhaps with some enamel damage, high relief features with wear. F meaning fine, of course does not mean fine, but considerable wear. Very good and good really mean the opposite. Therefore, a rule might be in buying items that you don't buy enameled pieces that aren't at least EF, unless they are rare, or an unenameled piece less than VF, again unless it's rare.

Europeans are more inclined to use a numbering system of Roman numerals I-V, but essentially they mean the same as above. Both systems will use a combination of terms such as VF/EF or III/II to show the condition of the obverse/reverse. In the case of a mounted group, the condition might be listed as VF-EF or II-III to show the range. To complicate matters even more, the word good, sometimes abbreviated as gd may be applied to EF, VF and F.

9

One thing that you may come across in a dealer's or auctioneer's catalogue is the dreaded "ek", not the German initials for the Eiserne Kreuz (the Iron Cross), but rather an "edge knock", where a medal has been knocked enough on the rim to create a dent. How serious this is will depend on the item involved, and the price.

As to enamel items, it is my opinion is that no damaged piece should be designated as EF or mint.

Mounted Groups

As will be seen in various photographs throughout this work there are a variety of ways in which a group of awards to a recipient can be mounted together. Each country has its own procedure for this, as well as designating the order of wearing based on the importance of each award, known as the Order of Precedence.

Wearing Orders, Medals and Decorations

Because we are so used to holding these items in our hands, or at least viewing them in some kind of display we may forget that Orders, medals and Decorations for the most part were worn by someone. The manner in which they were worn, the order in which they were worn has a bearing on how we might choose to display them ourselves.

The photographs appearing after this narrative show some examples of important personages wearing a variety of awards. These date primarily from the early 20th century and were chosen show just how intricate the whole matter could become.

First is the German Empress Augusta Victoria, consort of German Emperor William II. She is shown wearing a Royal Family Order, on the bow ribbon; the Johanniter Order (the Maltese Cross); and the breast star of the Order of the Black Eagle. She is also wearing a sash across her left shoulder.

Next is a portrait of King George VI of the United Kingdom of Great Britain and Ireland, and Emperor of India, in the uniform of Admiral of the Fleet of the Royal Navy. The photograph is c1914. He is wearing four breast stars, the maximum according to royal decree. Top is the Order of the Garter; below and to the left is the Order of the Bath; below and to the right is the Order of the Star of India; and below them is the Order of St Michael and St George. At the throat is the Grand Cross badge of the Order of the Bath. Around his neck is the Royal Victorian Chain. The King is also wearing a mounted group composed of breast badges of British Orders, as well as some foreign Orders including the French Legion of Honor. He wears the sash of the Order of the Garter over his left shoulder.

Third is Field Marshal Viscount Wolseley wearing the breast stars of the Order of St Patrick; the Bath, and St Michael and St George, plus another unidentifiable breast star, probably foreign. The sash badge can be seen hanging from a sash worn over the right shoulder. This photo is circa 1900, when he was Commander-in-Chief of the British Army. He is holding his Field Marshal's baton in his right hand.

Fourth is a picture of King Nicholas of Montenegro circa 1914. In native costume, he is wearing at the throat the Russian Orders of St George, and the Italian Military Order of Savoy. On his chest he has the breast star of the Danilo Order. On his bar he has among others the Orders of St Peter, and Danilo, and the Milosh Oblitch Medal.

Finally, there are two photographs of officers of the Imperial Russian Army and Navy showing differences in wearing style, and the variety of awards.

Lieut. General Schillinsky is shown wearing an interesting group of items. At top is a Russian breast star, not clearly identifiable. Underneath is the Grand Cross breast star of the Bulgarian Order of Military Merit. Below that is a breast star of the Chinese Order of the Double Dragon. On a bar he is wearing the Order of St Vladimir, probably the III Class and some other Imperial Russian medals. At his throat he is wearing the II Class badge of the Order of St Vladimir. On the right side of his tunic he is wearing three neck badges; the Order of St Anne II Class, the Order of St Stanislas II Class, and the French Legion of Honor III Class. This photograph shows the Russian Orders being worn without swords. It is circa 1914.

The last photograph is that of Vice Admiral Skridlov wearing his medal bar in a sloping fashion, considered naval or diplomatic style. On his "medal" bar among others there are the French Legion of Honor, and the Montenegrin Order of Danilo. The top breast star appears to be the Bulgarian Royal Military Order, and the lower the Order of St Vladimir. At the neck he wears the Order of St Vladimir II Class. This photograph is also circa 1914.

Military vs Civil Awards

Orders, Medals and decorations are frequently seen with swords attached to them. They may be crossed through the arms, at the top of the suspension, or even on the ribbon. The presence of swords can mean that this is a strictly military award, as in the case of the Military Merit Order of Bulgaria. It can mean as well that it was awarded to a member of the military, or that it has been given for being in combat.

The Bavarian Military Merit Order, and its attendant merit crosses is seen with and without swords, although commonly the former.

Miniature Medals

Sometime in the 19th century the practice of wearing smaller versions of Orders, Medals and Decorations came into vogue. For a variety of reasons it became inconvenient to wear the full size awards. Many

European, and some other countries, notably the United States, have almost abandoned the wearing of the full size awards, except on the most ceremonial occasions.

Miniature medals come in varying sizes. They are usually of the same metal as the originals. Miniature enameled orders can be exquisite. They are worn in a variety of ways. Sometimes they are worn on a brooch bar like the full size awards, sometimes from buttonhole devices, and also from miniature chains. The only major country not to use them was Russia, Imperial and Soviet. Sometimes they are awarded with the originals, or they may be obtained by private purchase. They are being collected, but do not have the same value as the originals.

Reverse of the Russian Order of St. Anne III Class showing the gold content hallmark "56" on the suspension ring.

British Order of the Bath Civil III Class, silver gilt, showing hallmarks.

Reverse of the 1914 Prussian Iron Cross I Class showing the 800 silver mark on the pin.

Top left - Anhalt Arts and Science Medal, oval. Top right - Hannoverian Waterloo Medal, round. Bottom left - British Military Cross, cross. Bottom right - Japanese Sacred Treasure 7th & 8th Class, "star".

Different Shapes

Top left - French Combat Merit Order. Top right - French "Cross" of July 1830. Bottom left - Latvian Gedeminas Order IV Class. Bottom right - Rumanian Air Force Bravery Order.

17

Different Shapes

Greek Order of Charity V Class

18

Different Shapes
Crosses

Top left - Austrian Military Merit Cross, Leopold cross. Top right - Prussian Iron Cross II Class 1914, cross pattée. Bottom left - Hohenzollern House Order, Rupert cross. Bottom right - Wuertemberg Wilhelm Cross II Class 1915, Rupert cross.

Top left - British Distinguished Service Order, Rupert cross. Top right - Greek Order of the Redeemer, Bath cross. Bottom left - Italian Order of Sts. Maurice & Lazarus, trefoil cross. Bottom right - Latvian Order of the Bearslayer, swastika.

Prussian Pour le Mérite, Maltese cross

Naming on American medals during WWII. Top left - Legion of Merit. Top right - Army Distinguished Service Medal. Bottom left - Navy Purple Heart (posthumous). Bottom right - Navy Good Conduct Medal.

Top left - United States WWI Victory Medal engraved on the obverse.
Bottom right - French fireman's medal engraved on reverse.

Top left - French lifesaving medal. Top right - French social service medal.
Bottom left - British 1914-15 Star. Bottom right - Italian Al Valore Militare.

Reverse of the United States Treasury Silver Lifesaving Medal.

Naming on the rim of American and British campaign medals. Left to right, US unofficially engraved, British impressed, British engraved, US Sampson Medal engraved, US Sampson Medal impressed.

German (Third Reich) award document of the 1939 II Class bar to the Prussian 1914 Iron Cross II Class.

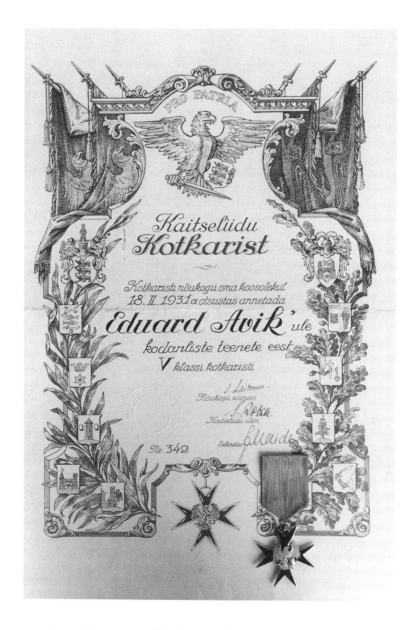

Award document of the Estonian Eagle Cross Order V Class.

German (Third Reich) award document of the German Cross signed by Admiral Dönitz.

Documents

French award certificate for the Croix de Guerre 1914-1918 named to an American.

Documents

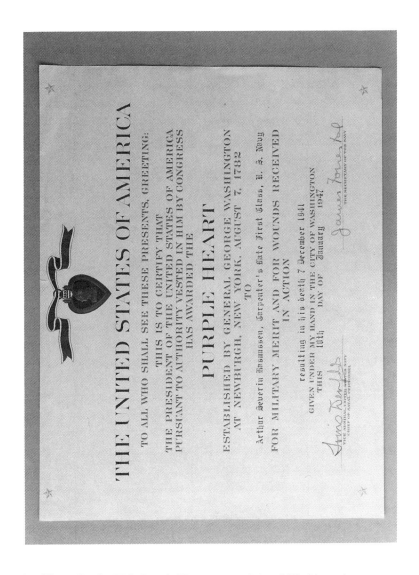

Certificate for the U.S. Purple Heart to a recipient killed in action
December 7, 1941.

31

CHIEF OF NAVAL OPERATIONS

       The Secretary of the Navy takes pride in presenting the NAVY COMMENDATION MEDAL posthumously to

GALE R. SIOW
AVIATION ELECTRONICS TECHNICIAN THIRD CLASS
UNITED STATES NAVY

for service as set forth in the following

CITATION:

       For meritorious achievement in aerial flight from 15 November 1967 to 11 January 1968 as a radioman flying in fixed-wing aircraft in Observation Squadron SIXTY-SEVEN. During this period, Petty Officer Siow participated in combat missions against preassigned targets in Southeast Asia. Due to the character of the operational missions, he was required to fly at low altitudes in an area where many active enemy automatic weapons and antiaircraft guns were emplaced. On 11 January 1968, the crew of which Petty Officer Siow was a member failed to return from one of these missions. His courage and devotion to duty in the face of extremely hazardous flying conditions were in keeping with the highest traditions of the United States Naval Service.

The Combat Distinguishing Device is authorized.

                     For the Secretary,

                     T. H. Moorer
                Admiral, United States Navy
                 Chief of Naval Operations

Citation for the U.S. Navy Commemdation Medal with combat "V".

Left - Belgian Leopold Order, Officer (Naval). Right - French Legion of Honor, Knight, Third Republic.

Prussian Order of the Crown I Class, Type II

United States Navy Mexican Service Medal 1911-1917 in issue box with ribbon bar.

Japanese award cases. Top - Lacquer style. Middle - Balsa. Bottom - Wood and cardboard.

Italian Order of Sts. Maurice Lazarus, Knight with miniature.

Top - Japan: Sacred Treasure, China 1894-1895, Russo-Japanese War.
Middle - Serbia: Retreat to Albania, Zeal Medal, Zeal Medal, 1912 Balkan
War, 1913 Balkan War Cross. Bottom - Multinational group: Norway-Olaf
Medal, Belgium-Royal Household Medal, Leopold II Medal, Russia-Zeal
Medal, Spain-Civil Merit Cross.

Top - British group: Military Cross, 1914-1918 War Medal, WWI Victory Medal. Middle - Imperial German group: Prussian Iron Cross II Class with 25 year Oakleaves, Saxon Albert Order, 1870-71 Campaign Medal with six bars, 1897 Wilhelm I Medal. Bottom - Imperial German Group: Bavarian Military Merit Cross, 1870-71 Campaign Medal, 1897 Wilhelm I Medal.

Top - United States Marine Corps group. Bottom - United States Coast Guard group.

German Empress Augusta Victoria, consort of German Emperor William II, wearing the Royal Family Order and the Johanniter Order on bow ribbons as well as the breast star of the Order of the Black Eagle.

King George VI of the United Kingdom of Great Britain and Ireland, and Emperor of India, in the uniform of Admiral of the Fleet of the Royal Navy. He is wearing four breast stars, the maximum according to royal decree. Top is the Order of the Garter; below and to the left is the Order of the Bath; below and to the right is the Order of the Star of India; and below them is the Order of St Michael and St George. At the throat is the Grand Cross badge of the Order of the Bath. Around his neck is the Royal Victorian Chain. The King is also wearing a mounted group composed of breast badges of British Orders. He wears the sash of the Order of the Garter over his left shoulder.

Field Marshal Viscount Wolseley wearing the breast stars of the Order of St. Patrick; the Bath, and St. Michael and St. George. This photo is circa 1900, when he was Commander-in-Chief of the British Army. He is holding his Field Marshal's baton in his right hand.

King Nicholas of Montenegro in native costume. He is wearing at the throat the Russian Orders of St George, and the Italian Military Order of Savoy. On his chest he has the breast star of the Danilo Order. His bar he has among others the Order of St. Peter, the Order of Danilo and the Milosh Oblitch Medal.

44

Ген.-Лейт. Я. Г. ЖИЛИНСКİЙ.

Russian Lieut. General Schillinsky circa 1914. He is wearing the breast stars of the Bulgarian Order of Military Merit and Chinese Order of the Double Dragon. On the right side of his tunic are three neck badges; the Order of St Anne II Class, the Order of St Stanislas II Class, and the French Legion of Honor III Class.

45

Russian Vice Admiral Skridlov wearing his medal bar in a sloping fashion, considered naval or diplomatic style. On the bar, among others, are the French Legion of Honor and the Montenegrin Order of Danilo. The top breast star is the Bulgarian Royal Military Order and below is the Order of St. Vladimir. At the neck he wears the Order of St Vladimir II Class. This photograph is also circa 1914.

Top left - Prussian Order of the Red Eagle IV Class with swords, type III on Iron Cross ribbon. Bottom right - Order of the Red Eagle, type II without swords on civil ribbon.

Top left - Bulgarian Military Merit Order. Top right - Bulgarian Civil Merit Order. Bottom left - Belgian Order of Leopold, military knight with swords. Bottom right - Belgian Order of Leopold, civil knight without swords.

Top - Multinational miniature group worn on chain. Middle - British mounted miniature group. Bottom - Full size British group for comparison.

Top - United States Navy miniature group. Bottom - Full size group for comparison.

CHAPTER I

COLLECTING ORDERS, MEDALS & DECORATIONS

There have always been the few collectors who have been interested in awards granted by some monarch or government for heroism, long service, military campaigns and the like, but only recently have these items become the focus of a popular hobby. Since the early 1960's the collecting of these awards has grown steadily, and the value of many of them have grown accordingly.

The practice of making awards for gallantry and various other distinctions for military and civilian service dates largely from the late 18th & early 19th centuries. Napoleon Bonaparte was keenly aware that some token of recognition from his country could be a great spur to achievement. The Legion of Honor was the result. Unlike pre-revolutionary France where privilege, rank and class determined everything, it became possible for any Frenchman to aspire to this coveted award. Since its founding in 1802, the Legion of Honor has been bestowed on thousands of French citizens, military and civilian, as well as on many foreigners. Besides France, Great Britain, Austria and the German States awarded many such distinctions in the same time period and later. Strictly speaking the field can be broken down into three broad categories.

1. ORDERS - Orders originally date back to the days of knighthood in the Middle Ages, implying both an association with the noble class of society and a religious ideal. Some of the oldest of these Orders are: The Order of the Garter (Great Britain), Dannebrog (Denmark) and the Annunciation (Savoy-Italy). However, today they reflect mainly special distinctions conferred on citizens for some type of service in peace or war, both civil and military. Naturally, no communist country would accept the notion that its Orders had any noble or religious origins.

Orders may come in any grouping of one to five classes, although some countries like Japan may have them with more. Class one, often referred to as the Grand Cross, will normally consist of a large metal and enameled breast star, worn on the left side of the chest, and a large, wide ribbon, called a sash, worn across the chest, over one shoulder, with a metal and enameled badge hanging from it. The term badge in this context will mean that part of an Order that hangs from a ribbon, and is usually enameled metal. Class two normally will consist of a smaller badge hanging from a ribbon worn around the neck, and a smaller breast star. This class goes by several names; Knight Commander (Great Britain), Grand Officer, Commander I Class, Commander with star. Class three is normally the neck badge alone, being referred to as Commander or Commander II Cl.

Class four is worn on the left chest on a ribbon, and usually referred to as the Officer class. In some countries the fourth class may also have a ribbon device called a rosette. The Fifth class is usually similar in appearance as the fourth, but usually of a different metal, but worn in the same manner, and referred to as Knight (in Great Britain as member).

The metals used may include from gold, silver, and bronze, with most badges enameled, while some are gold plated or gilt. Badges frequently are in cross form, while the breast star will have from four to eight points.

Many references use the term gold when they mean gold colored or gold-plated, which may in turn mean silver/gilt or bronze/gilt. In Germany and Austria the word golden was often used in this manner. Where possible I have tried to indicate whether the item was actually gold, but this was not always possible. Additionally, the term silver sometimes means silver color or silver plate. Obviously, the term "gold/gilt" should not be used, but something silver plated may be described as "silvered".

2. DECORATIONS-This is a common, all inclusive term frequently used to describe the whole field, but the word more properly refers to an award, other than an Order, and given for some special distinction such as for heroism against the enemy in combat. Examples of these might be the British Victoria Cross, and the U.S.A.'s Medal of Honor, each their country's highest valor award. Some decorations may be made of gold or silver, some enameled. The Victoria Cross is made of bronze from captured Russian cannon taken in the Crimean War 1854-56. Some countries such as Imperial Russia, Great Britain, and Prussia have had separate bravery awards for officers and enlisted men. The famous Prussian Pour Le Mérite was only for officers; enlisted men received the far less known Military Merit Cross.

3. MEDALS-This term is used mistakenly more than any other to describe the whole field. Most properly it should be applied to any gold, silver or bronze metal award hanging from a ribbon, usually not enameled, and issued to commemorate a whole range of military campaigns, long service, royal occasions, independence celebrations, or the like. It should be pointed out that the terms "decorations" and "medals" are often used interchangeably, and a precise definition to please everyone does not exist.

For the new collector there seems to be a bewildering number of items available, a great lack of information on these same items, and how to proceed. How do you as the novice collector go about your hobby? Before you do anything else buy or borrow books, and soon you will begin to have some ideas on the subject. Of course you might wonder where do you find out about what books to obtain. Later on in this work you will find an extensive bibliography to guide your steps. After you have done some reading what do you do next? There are many possibilities! What is also of great value is to be able to find a more advanced collector who is willing to listen to and answer many questions. In the field of collecting a mentor can advance your knowledge, and accelerate your progress as a collector.

However, you must decide which is the way to collect. It is my form belief that there is no correct way, only different ways! Whatever pleases you is correct, although considering some advice doesn't hurt, and may help. Here are some possibilities:

1. You can decide to have a representative, worldwide collection. Thus, you will try to get an item from as many countries in the world as you can. The chief advantage is that you won't have to spend too much money. The chief disadvantages are that you won't have too much focus to your collection, and obtaining information on your items may be difficult.

2. You can collect Orders of the world, This is a variation of the above, but is more costly, as Orders are likely to be higher in price and rarer. However, since you will have a grouping of enameled awards there will be a more pleasing appearance to your collection.

3. Collecting gallantry awards from around the world can be very satisfying, but some of these are going to be expensive.

4. Collecting military campaign medals is a particularly interesting approach. The history of many countries can be seen in this way, and with the exception of some of the British and American items, the cost will not be too high.

5. Collecting lifesaving medals can be very interesting to those fascinated by non-combat heroism. These awards have been issued by many countries, for more than a hundred years.

6. Many countries have made Red Cross awards which can form the basis for a very interesting collection.

7. Long Service Medals have been issued by many countries, and represent another possible avenue of approach.

8. Royal occasion awards such as weddings, jubilees, coronations have a great appeal, and offer an international approach to collecting.

9. Collecting topically also is possible. You can choose from such subjects as: Napoleonic era; Boxer Rebellion; World War I; World War II; Korean War; Independence Medals or anything else which catches your interest.

10. Collecting by country is a very common approach. The most popular countries for collector interest seem to be the U.S.A., Great Britain, Germany till 1945, Austria till 1918, and Imperial Russia. As the awards of these countries are more popular their prices are likely to be higher.

However, since the collapse of the Soviet Union, and the appearance of awards from that country at considerably lower prices, plus the publication of some references, we may see a new popular field for the collector. Although, it takes time to see whether something like this is a fad, or if there is going to be a sustainable, and more sophisticated approach.

To concentrate their efforts more easily, some collectors break down the country concept. Thus, a collector might collect only British Military Campaign Medals. This could be refined even further by staying with only one unit or regiment of the British army. Since most British campaign medals are named to the recipient it is possible to research the history of the man and the medal together.

The awards of the United States include an array of campaign and service medals from the Civil War to the present, as well as numerous ones for meritorious and long service, plus an extensive system of gallantry awards for the armed forces. The various departments, component and separate agencies of the Federal Government agencies have also issued many decorations. It might also be mentioned that there are many awards from the several states dating back to the Mexican War of the 1840's, predating those of the Federal Government.

The awards system of Great Britain is not only comprehensive but awesome in its scope. Many collectors favor British items not only because of their beauty and integrity, but also because so many of them have the recipient's name on them, which enables the collector to do much research. Literature on British awards is extensive and collectors gladly exchange information.

The German States till 1918 issued many items covering major conflicts in history, which in themselves lend a topical approach to collecting. The III Reich section is also very extensive, as this an area of great collector interest. However, it is also the most dangerous field of collecting due to the vast amount of fakes on the market.

The Orders, medals, and decorations of Imperial Russia are especially impressive. The Orders except for a brief period in World War I were genuine gold, with superb enamel work. The campaign medals are perhaps the oldest series stretching from the days of Peter the Great in the early 18th century, to Nicholas II in the early 20th century.

A major problem any collector must face is money. Like any other collectible field, this comes into play very quickly. How much should you spend? How much is something worth? In the third edition of my book **VERNON'S COLLECTORS' GUIDE TO ORDERS, MEDALS AND DECORATIONS (with valuations)**, I attempt to answer the latter question. Only you can really decide how much you can afford to spend. Focus your collecting so that you can obtain the best value for what you spend. You must decide whether you want a large number of items which are modest in cost or a few items that are expensive.

You must bear in mind that cost or value is going to depend on a variety of factors. The dealer's cost, rarity and desirability (collector interest) should always be taken into consideration. There are rare items that do not command high prices because the collector interest in that country's awards is not very great.

I would say that whenever possible, you buy the best piece you can afford, and in the best condition. If you pass up common items their price may increase somewhat, but they will be easily obtainable. However, if you pass up a rare piece not only may the price go up , but it will be difficult to obtain when you want it. Remember: the higher the class of the award, the higher the price. They were given more sparingly, and are more valuable. Gold items are valuable because of intrinsic worth. A gold medal may weigh a lot but a gold order is likely to be hollow, and not nearly as valuable as you might think. A badly damaged enameled order, unless it is very rare, can be worth a lot less than one in excellent, undamaged condition. The few very rare pieces are the exception.

I have been asked many times about investment possibilities in this field. The only way to answer this is to indicate that like any collectible field there are always possibilities of appreciation in value of the items you buy. However, this is a hobby that depends heavily on whim and changing interests. The best approach is to collect what you can afford, and what interests you. If there is appreciation in the value of the items you have bought over the years so much the better for you. If there have been no changes or even a decline in value then you have the satisfaction of enjoying your hobby.

During a recent time of high international inflation, many orders and decorations, like other collectibles, soared in value as speculators came into the field. However, the day of reckoning came, and the British market in particular suffered spectacular declines. The collector should understand that the great variations in the value of the U.S. dollar has caused great changes in values in both directions. Finally, I would point out that collector interest changes, so some items fall out of favor causing prices to decline, while others gain favor causing prices to rise.

There comes a time when the collector contemplates selling all or part of his/her collection. Should you wish to sell to a dealer you will have to consider the following. No dealer is going to give you retail value. How would there be any profit involved? Depending on the items you are offering you can expect 25% to 50% of retail on common material, with perhaps 60% on better items, from a dealer. Of course you have the right to ask any price you desire, but there is no obligation on the dealers' part to pay it! If you sell a whole collection you must realize that the inclusion of much common material will cause the dealer to hedge his offer, in order to protect himself being stuck with a large number of pieces that are difficult to sell.

You can offer your items in an auction. This has the possible advantage of obtaining higher prices, but there are the auctioneers' fees to pay, and there is no guarantee that your item will sell at a price that will please you, or even be sold at all. Furthermore, settlement of your deal may take more time than you wish.

You as the collector can always try to sell the collection at retail, like a dealer. However, it is likely to be a piecemeal approach, with the best pieces going first. Moreover, you should bear in mind that if you try to get the highest possible prices for your items you may find considerable resistance on the part of other collectors. It is all very well for the seller to say that something is worth such and such, but nothing is worth anything more than someone is willing to pay. Unless the value you place on an item you are selling is acceptable to a buyer then there is no sale!

I believe that collecting in this field, as in any other, should be based on how much enjoyment a person can get out of it, rather than worry about future value. If your collection increases in value, then the enjoyment is even greater. People who began their collecting before the mid-1960's saw many of their items go up in value enormously, but were in many cases. Yet were unable to come to grips with the fact that if their items were worth more, then they could not expect to buy them at the bargain prices of the "good old days" when few people collected. Orders, medals and decorations were once cheap because hardly anyone was interested in them. Growth in the number of collectors has meant higher prices.

However, when prices go too high, many collectors will be frozen out of the market. This happened, and in response prices came down, and more people resumed collecting.

United States Combat Gallantry Awards

Top left - Army Distinguished Service Cross. Top right - Navy Cross.
Bottom left - Silver Star. Bottom right - Bronze Star with valor "V".

57

Top left - French Valor Cross. Top right - British Victoria Cross (copy). Bottom left - Belgian Croix de Guerre with palms. Bottom right - Serbian Milosh Oblitch Medal.

Top left - Russian St. George Cross IV Class. Top right - Soviet Order of Glory III Class. Bottom left- Bavarian Military Merit Cross II Class with Swords. Bottom right - French Médaille Militaire 1870.

Top left - British George Cross (copy). Top right - French lifesaving medal, Napoleon III. Bottom left - United States Soldier's Medal. Bottom right - United States Navy-Marine Corps Medal.

Top left - British Army of India Medal 1799-1826. Top right - French Mexican Campaign Medal 1862-1863. Bottom left - United States Navy Civil War Medal 1861-1865. Bottom right - Bavarian Austrian War Cross 1866.

Top left - British India General Service Medal 1854-1895. Top right - Prussian Treuen Kriegern Cross 1866. Bottom left - French Indo China Medal 1883-1885. Bottom right - United States Army Indian Wars Medal.

Campaign Medals

Right - United States Navy West Indies Naval Campaign Medal (Sampson Medal), chain link type. Top right - German Boxer Rebellion Medal 1900-1901 (combattent). Bottom right - United States Army China Campign Medal 1900-1901.

Top - Spanish Medal of the Philippines 1896-1898. Bottom left - United States Army Philippine Campaign Medal 1898-1903. Bottom right - United States Navy Philippine Campaign Medal 1899-1903.

Top left - French WWII Commemorative Medal with campaign bars. Top right - Soviet Defense of the Caucasus Medal. Bottom left - United States European, African, Middle Eastern Campaign Medal. Bottom right - Philippine Liberation Medal.

Campaign Medals

Top left - British Korean Service Medal 1950-1953. Top right - French Suez Canal Campaign Medal 1956. Bottom left - United States Vietnam Service Medal. Bottom right - Italian Sinai Peace Keeping Medal.

66

Top - Bulgaria. Left - Austria Hungary. Right - Hungary. Bottom - Serbia
Balkan War 1912-1913.

CHAPTER II

COPIES, FAKES & REPRODUCTIONS

In any collecting field, the collector faces a problem, as to whether the material being offered or bought is genuine. The term employed for an item which not original may depend on the intent of the maker with regard to how it is to be disposed of. If there were no intent to defraud then the term copy (or reproduction) is correct.

However, if as is often the case the purpose was or is to deceive the collector then the proper term is fake. In **VERNON'S COLLECTORS' GUIDE TO ORDERS, MEDALS, AND DECORATIONS** I tried to indicate special problems of copies and fakes throughout the value section, recognizing in the last analysis that the two terms are really the same I use the word copy for convenience. I have tried also to indicate in the introduction to each country where some special problem may exist.

The greatest number of copies on the market today are those of III Reich awards. Without quoting an actual percentage, it is likely that much of the material being offered either is not genuine or at least questionable. Some is very obvious, while much may be excellent in appearance, and difficult to decide about. One German dealer told me copies were being made in Austria as early as 1946, and in Germany in 1947. Initially, old dies were used to restrike new items. Then new dies were made up. Most of the original material found in the U.S.A. derives from it being brought back by the returned World War II veteran. However, if he was in the Army of Occupation after the war, he may have inadvertently picked up pieces that were restrikes or copies.

Nevertheless, none of this is meant to imply that the collector cannot find genuine Nazi awards, only that greater care must be taken.

Identifying genuine III Reich awards is not always easy. Some restrikes produced after World War II from original dies are virtually indistinguishable from original items. Many pieces may seem to be in poor condition because as the war ground on the quality of the materials used and/or the workmanship deteriorated. Thus, it is quite possible that an original item can have a poor quality appearance, while that well-made piece could be a copy. Much III Reich material is hallmarked in some way. You may see numbers such 800 or 900 to indicate silver content. Letters such as R.K. or R.S., or names like Juncker, and Peekhaus refer to a manufacturer. "L"-prefixed numbers such as L/11 will refer to a maker also, as will the plain number 21. There is controversy over the letters RS which indicate the maker Rudolf Souval of Vienna Austria. One may see two types of letters, one rounded, and one angular. There is a difference of opinion as to which is used on genuine material.

I must emphasize the mere appearance of a hallmark or number on a III Reich item is no guarantee of its being genuine; nor is the absence of such mean that you have a copy. III Reich medals are frequently marked on the ribbon ring, while badges may be marked on the reverse, or on top of or underneath the pin.

On the badges you should examine the pin and catch carefully. If there is any sign of epoxy glue then the piece has either been repaired, or it is a fake, since epoxy did not exist in World War II. Some badges have been copied in lead. If you can bend it easily and write with it then you have a copy. If there are signs of bubbling and pitting, and the surface is not clearly struck, you may have a casting rather than a die struck item. Originals were rarely produced in this manner. Of course, there are die struck copies.

Certainly, one of the most famous awards in the world is the Iron Cross, so named because of its main component. Thus, a test of a World War II Iron Cross (in all classes) should be as to whether it is magnetic or not. There are those who say that there were some late World War II pieces that weren't so made, but my feeling is that they are to be avoided.

Another frequently copied piece is the so-called "Blue Max", the Prussian Officers' bravery award the Pour Le Mérite. Instituted in the 18th century, it has appeared in many types and styles, as well as in gold, silver/gilt and bronze/gilt. While there have been copies of the early items most collectors will come across the World War I period pieces, and it is these which pose the most problems. The fact that a piece is gold with a hallmark is no guarantee of its being genuine.

What complicates the matter even further, is that some recipients, in order to protect this coveted award from wear, had wearing copies made by an official jeweler. These copies have an acceptable status in the collector world below that of the originals, but far above the host of low quality items made after World War II. There are very nice quality copies made in Vienna between the wars which will also command a respectable place in a collection. Consulting reference materials is essential in this matter. A final note on III Reich hallmarks. It is generally accepted that the mark of L/58 is an indication of the item being a post-World War II copy, of high quality perhaps, but a copy nevertheless.

British awards present fewer, but different types of problems. There are copies of some British awards, made in France after World War I, namely, the Military Medal and the Distinguished Service Medal-George V type, but they are fairly obvious. They have no designer's name on the obverse, they don't swivel at the suspension, and they are unnamed. Others such as the Edward VI Distinguished Conduct Medal, the George V Distinguished Service Order, and the George VI Distinguished Flying Cross present more of a problem.

Fortunately for the collector these and other items are covered in Purves-**COLLECTING MEDALS & DECORATIONS** and in Abbott & Tamplin-**BRITISH GALLANTRY AWARDS**. Unnamed copies of the Victoria Cross are common. It can be said with reasonable assurance that an unnamed Victoria Cross is a copy since awarded ones were always named. There may be exceptions in the case of those presented to museums, or those awarded to the Unknown Soldiers of the First World War, from other countries. Despite this, the V.C. does not present a problem for most collectors as its price is very high. The Air Force Cross is a tricky item indeed. Care must be taken that the monarch's cipher is the same on the obverse and reverse, and that the designer's initials appear in the 7 o'clock position on the obverse centre.

The major problem which occurs with British awards is with the naming of the campaign medals, especially where the name of the original recipient has been ground off and replaced by someone else's. This renaming may have been done to deceive collectors, or simply by a recipient who lost his medal(s), and wanted to replace it (them). There are a few instances of medals being officially renamed. In these verifiable cases the medals have the same value as an unaltered piece. Another, less prevalent, problem is that of fake bars to make relatively common medals into rarer ones. The naming of otherwise unnamed medals also can present a problem. Some years ago a number of unnamed medals from the Crimean War with the bar Balaklava were named up to members of units which took part in the classic "Charge of the Light Brigade". These pieces, seemingly named in the correct style, were at first accepted as genuine. Only the sharp eyes of a British dealer discovered minute differences in the naming that revealed that these pieces were frauds.

The faking of American medals involves several different problems. There have been three basic numbering systems used to number U.S. campaign medals, with several variations. There are genuine unnumbered medals that have faked numbering. The only real protection against this is experience, and being able to compare a medal with another, known, original piece. More details on the numbering systems will be found in the U.S. section.

Several years ago a flood of U.S. Navy and Marine Corps campaign medals came on the market, presumably made somewhere in the Orient. They are identifiable by their dark appearance, fuzzy detail, and a little knob instead of the normal ring. Moreover, some of these have been seen with rings instead of knobs. Nevertheless, these pieces look poor and should not fool anyone if carefully examined.

Copies have been made in many countries, especially in France, Germany, and Austria, but also in the U.S.A., Britain, and in S.E. Asia. Much III Reich material has come from the U.S.A. as well as Europe. The chief sources for much of the other material seems to have been Paris and Vienna. The makers at one time may have been official suppliers of awards to governments and royal houses, and continued to make them after the awarding authorities either no longer existed, or no longer had the undisputed right to continue awarding them.

Many of these items are of good or even excellent quality, yet should be regarded as copies, or at best of doubtful parentage. Without being able

70

to know when an item was made the collector can face a complicated problem. Here is where hallmarks can be of assistance. Consult **COURT JEWELERS OF THE WORLD** by Jeffrey Jacob.

An important step is getting as much reference material as possible. The best protection a collector can have against the pitfalls of collecting is as many books as possible. There is no such thing as spending too much on research materials when you balance it against the high cost of ignorance. It is probable that you will find references will have overlapping information. There is no one work which has everything in it.

When you realize that collectors are prepared to spend large sums of money on pieces for a collection, yet hesitate to part with say fifty dollars for a book which could save them many times its cost, it is not surprising that these same people are taken advantage of. Every collector should buy as many books as possible before going into this field in a serious way.

Study your references, ask questions of the seller, pick up items and examine them carefully with a powerful magnifier. In your collecting you need to be a wise consumer also. As a buyer you have no obligation to buy at, but sometimes a "bargain" is hard to resist. If you appear to know what you are doing then you will be prepared to impress the seller. He of course is under no obligation to sell to you at a particular price, just because you would like him to.

Very often you will find that when you are buying from someone who does not normally handle this material there can be a great variation in price. You may be offered a rare item at a low price, and conversely a high price on a common item. A clear example of this the New York State Shooting Badge, once made by Tiffany & Co. of New York. Some antique dealers assume that since it is a Tiffany piece that it has a great deal of value, whereas in reality the badge is very common and commands about $15.00.

During the course of your collecting the question is going to arise whether to buy copies. My personal inclination is not to do so. However, this is a matter which you have to decide in relation to the type of collection that you want. If you are collecting gallantry awards you may well be satisfied with paying $25.00 for an excellent copy of a Victoria Cross rather than $20,000.00 for an original. I have known a collector to pay $1000.00 for a copy set of the I Class of the Imperial Russian Order of St George, virtually unobtainable as an original, and certainly astronomical in cost.

Copies run in all sorts of price ranges, and unless the item is extremely rare should be avoided. The more copies you have in your collection, the poorer impression it will make. You might even depreciate the value of the genuine pieces that you have which may be judged by the company they keep. There is enough original material around to be collected. Nevertheless, you must be the final judge.

The German Cross in Gold. Note the greater detail in the wreath and thicker arms of the swastika in the original at top as compared with the fake below.

Reverse of the German Cross. The original on top has rivets while the fake at bottom does not.

The Russian St. George Cross in silver. Note the difference in the suspension of the original at top as compared with the fake below (which is a Prussian style piece).

Reverse of the Russian St. George Cross in Silver. The original at top is marked with the grade of the award on the lower arm while the fake below is not.

Genuine rim numbering on United States campaign medals.

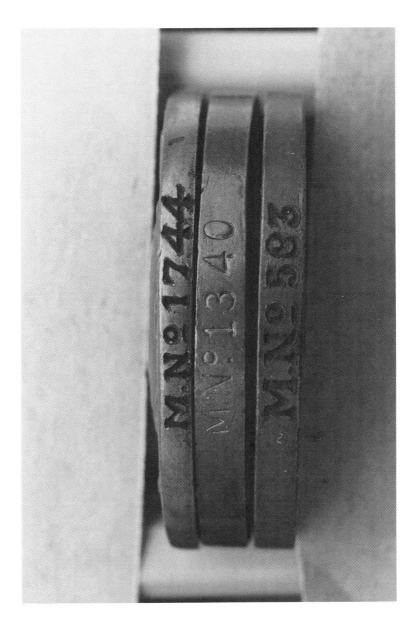

Fake numbering on United States campaign medals. The numbering on the outer medals is engraved, not stamped. The numbering on the center medal is stamped but lacks serifs on the M and N in "M.No.".

United States Navy Philippine Campaign Medal. Notice the differences in suspension and detail on the originals at top as compared with the fakes below.

CHAPTER III

RIBBON STYLES

Since many collectors stay with the awards of one country they become familiar with them, their mountings, their ribbon types etc. However, most collectors eventually come across awards from other countries that they may know nothing about and seek to find out some basic information. While it is not possible to provide information from every single country included in this book it is possible to give some general guidelines which may help.

Most collectors readily understand that a medal etc hangs from a ribbon. What collectors are not prepared for is the great variation in the styles of ribbon worn. Breast decorations awards of Austria and Hungary are seen on a triangular ribbon, but so are the awards of Serbia, Montenegro, Yugoslavia, Bulgaria, and amazingly enough the Order of the Sacred Treasure of Japan in the classes of IV-VIII.

The breast awards of Imperial Russia are seen on a unique five sided ribbon. British campaign medals mainly are suspended from ribbons which hang in a straight manner, unlike those of the U.S.A. which are gathered at the bottom to go through a ring.

German awards from the various time periods can have several types of ribbons, which may depend on their mounting. German and British awards are frequently found mounted in groups, again with various types of ribbon arrangements. When mounted in a group, these awards will have some kind of pin on the back to facilitate wearing on the uniform.

What perplexes many collectors is how the "medal" is worn on the uniform. All awards from the U.S.A. come with a brooch on the ribbon for wearing. Most items from other countries do not appear to have such. Many French awards come with a "U" shaped device with sharp points for sticking into the uniform. Frequently these stick into the fingers of the collector, although there is no evidence that any government planned this deliberately. Some collectors sew safety pins on the back of the ribbons for mounting. Others fasten a small piece of cardboard on the ribbon back and put a thumb tack through it onto the surface of the display case.

If you do decide to display your items in cases be very careful about keeping them out of the direct rays of sunlight which can cause enamel to crack or smash, and ribbons to fade. Ribbon material has also changed over the years.

Originally many ribbons were silk, and then later cotton, but in recent years they have been rayon and nylon. Some collectors want only original ribbons on their medal even if very tattered, even though no serving soldier or official would have been permitted to appear wearing such.

In a few cases the ribbon may be rarer than the medal it hangs from. A good example of this is the French medal for Mexico 1862-63, which has an embroidered eagle and snake. Later editions of the ribbon are printed instead.

Mention can be made on some of the devices that may be found on the ribbons of awards. This will be elaborated further on in this book, with some illustrations. Many countries use a rosette (a circular piece of cardboard covered with ribbon) on the ribbon of the fourth class of an Order to denote that class. This is a French origination, but can be found on the Austrian style ribbon of Bulgaria and on the Orders of Japan.

What sometimes confuses collectors that some awards have more than one ribbon, one for peacetime and one for wartime. Some may have the same ribbon for a military or civil award, while some may differentiate in a simple manner. The British Order of the Bath is a good example of how to confuse the collector. The ribbons are identical for the military and civil divisions, as are the breast stars with the exception of a wreath on the military type. However, the military badges are completely different.

The British Empire Order went through a complete change in the 1930's, with ribbon and design. The type II ribbon could be worn with the type I design, although not the reverse. Also in both types the only difference between the military and civil awards is that a vertical stripe would be found in the centre of the ribbon. In the case of Rumania in the 1930's several of its Orders were changed in design, as were the ribbons.

The actual wearing of awards varies from country to country. The usual practice consists of the highest class being having a broad ribbon (sash) worn over one shoulder, across the chest, with a large metal and enameled badge hanging from it, with a large metal, commonly enameled, plaque or breast star of four to eight points worn on the left chest.

Some of the Orders have with their highest class a Chain or Collar of precious metal and enamel, with the Order badge hanging from it. The second class usually consists of badge hanging from a narrower ribbon, referred to as a neck ribbon, cravat, or necklet, around the neck, with a smaller breast star also worn on the left chest. The III Class will be worn around the neck, while the fourth and lower classes will be worn on an even narrower ribbon on the left chest.

For some awards the I Class will be worn only around the neck . Some have only one class altogether; and for some the term I Class may mean a pin back award as in the case of the Iron Cross I Class, worn pinback on the left chest without a ribbon.

A decision often faced by collectors is whether to buy medals that don't have ribbons, or have the wrong one. While this is a matter of individual choice I would point out that replacement ribbons are obtainable, and that we are collecting medals, not ribbons.

Top left to right - Japan (reverse), Soviet Russia, Imperial Russia. Bottom left to right - Austria, United States, Great Britain.

Top - Bulgarian Civil Merit Order. Middle - Croatian Merit Order (Muslim Type). Bottom - Japanese Showa Enthronement medal.

Top left - Serbian Red Cross Order on ladies' bow. Top right - Austro-Hungarian Leopold Order, Knight. Bottom left - Vietnamese Army Distinguished Service Order, I Class. Bottom right - British China 1900.

United States Navy Medal of Honor. Top left - 1944 type on neck ribbon.
Bottom right - Civil War type on breast ribbon (copy).

United States campaign medal brooches. Top left - Split wrap, navy early 1900's. Top right - Full wrap, army early 1900's. Bottom left - Slot brooch, World War II. Bottom right - crimped brooch, World War II and later.

Soviet ribbon varieties. Top - Ushakhov medal. Bottom left - Distinguished Labor Service, type I. Bottom right - Order of the Patriotic War, type I.

Variations of the Order of Honor (Badge of Honor). Bottom left - Type I with early ribbon. Top left - Type II without ribbon, screw back. Right - Type III with current ribbon.

Ribbonless to ribbon. Top - Soviet Order of Lenin, type II without ribbon, screw back. Bottom - Order of Lenin, type III with ribbon.

Ribbon to ribbonless. Top - Soviet Order of Alexander Nevsky, type I with early ribbon. Bottom - Type II without ribbon, screw back.

CHAPTER IV

ORDERS OF KNIGHTHOOD

In effect the whole field we are speaking of began with Orders of Knighthood, which trace back their origin to the Crusades in the late Middle Ages. Many of the crusaders were gentlemen of noble birth who dedicated their lives to both god and the sword. Thus, they were a select group who wore distinctive clothing, and insignia. In time these insignia became refined in metal and enameled badges, stars, plaques, or whatever one cares to call them.

With some exceptions Orders came in one of three styles. In one class (usually the highest Order of a country) in three classes, or in five classes. The Chinese Golden Grain in nine classes, the Japanese Rising Sun in eight classes, to name only two, are examples of the exceptions.

The Orders of Great Britain clearly show these three styles. Orders of the Garter, Thistle, St Patrick are one class. The Order of the Bath is a three class Order, while the British Empire Order, and the Royal Victorian Order have five classes.

The names of the classes vary depending on the practice or usage of the country concerned. In some cases the French naming style is used, in others the German naming style.

A one class order usually consists of an enameled badge of silver or gold, hanging from a wide ribbon called a sash, worn across the chest, over one shoulder. Accompanying it is a breast star of four to eight points, worn on the left breast.

A three class order usually consists of the highest class, as above, most often called the Grand Cross, in Great Britain Knight Grand Cross, and occasionally known as the I Class. The next highest class will have a similar badge to the Grand Cross, but smaller, with a different suspension, worn around the neck on a ribbon, with a similar or smaller breast star on the left breast. The third class will usually consist of the second class badge worn on its own.

A clear example of a different configuration is shown by the Order of the Iron Crown Of Austria-Hungary, a three class Order, which consisted of the highest class, the Grand Cross, sash, badge and breast star; the Commander neck badge, and the Knight, breast badge.

To create a five class order there would be added a fourth class or Officer, worn on the left breast, suspended from a ribbon, a smaller, enameled gold or silver/gilt badge; while the fifth class would be similar to the fourth, but most often silver and enamel.

The above designations are not universal, although they apply to most Orders of European, and European influenced countries. They do not apply to the Orders of communist countries, which had their own reason for being.

In Great Britain only the two highest grades of Orders are identified with the word "knight" as they conferred the non-hereditary title of "Sir" before the recipient's name. To complicate the matter even further the British system of awards allows letters to be appended to a person's last name who has been granted an Order. See the section on Great Britain for elaboration of this matter.

The foundation of the modern orders system may be traced to the French Legion of Honor, and its five classes. Thus, those countries following the French style of naming classes used the terminology of Grand Cross for Class I, Grand Officer for Class II, Commander for Class III, Officer for Class IV, and Knight for Class V.

Many countries have followed the practice of placing a rosette, a circular ribbon covered piece of metal or cardboard, on the ribbon of the IV Class to show that it is the fourth rather than the fifth class. In some cases without this rosette there is no distinction in appearance of the IV and V classes. A good example of this is the Order of the Crown of Italy, whose IV and V classes are identical except for the ribbon rosette on the IV Class. Some countries distinguish between the IV and V classes by the metal used; the IV Class being of gold/enamel, or silver/gilt/enamel, and the V being silver/enamel, an example of this being the Greek Order of the Phoenix.

In the British Orders system there are only two five class orders, the Royal Victorian Order, and the British Empire Order. In those Orders the IV Classes are referred to as Lieutenant, and Officer respectively, and the V Classes as Member. In addition the Orders of the Bath, military and civil, and Sts Michael and George refer to their III Class as Companion, while the Royal Victorian Order, and the British Empire Order refer to their III Class as Commander.

Breast Stars. Top - Serbian Order of the White Eagle. Middle - French Legion of Honor. Bottom left - Danish Order of Dannebrog. Bottom right- Estonian Order of the White Star.

Reverse of the opposite page. Note the variety in styles of manufacture.

Breast Stars. Top - Brazilian Order of the Rose. Bottom - Rumanian Order of Carol.

Breast Stars. Top - Montenegro, Order of Danilo. Middle - Japan, Order of the Rising Sun. Bottom - Slovakia, Order of Prince Pribina.

Breast Stars. Top - Turkey, Order of the Medjidie. Middle - France, Order of the Dragon of Annam. Bottom - Thailand (Siam) Order of the Crown.

German Orders. Top left - Hannover, Order of Ernst-August, Knight. Top right - Oldenburg, Order of Peter Frederick Louis, Knight. Bottom left - Saxony, Albert Order, Knight I Class. Bottom right - Saxe-Weimar, Order of the Falcon, Knight.

Top - Estonia, Order of the White Star, V Class. Bottom left - Luxembourg, Order of Adolph, Knight. Bottom right - Montenegro, Order of Danilo, Knight.

Top - Rumania, Order of Michael the Brave, Knight. Bottom left - Russia, Order of St. George, IV Class. Bottom right - Serbia, Order of the White Eagle, Knight.

Belgian Order of Leopold, Grand Cross.

Belgian Order of Leopold. Top - Grand Officer Star. Left - Officer. Right - Knight. Bottom - Commander.

Top left - Austrian Order of the Iron Crown, III Class. Bottom right-
Austrian Order of Franz Joseph, Knight.

Tinsel Star. Sicily, Order of St. Ferdinand.

CHAPTER V

AWARDS BY COUNTRIES OR TOPICS

The countries listed below are to be found in **VERNON'S COLLECTORS' GUIDE TO ORDERS, MEDALS, AND DECORATIONS (with valuations)**-third edition.

ALBANIA
Principality 1914; Kingdom 1920's; Italian Occupation 1939; People's Republic after World War II.

The Orders and awards of this obscure European country can be divided into three phases. Phase I coincides with the extension of German influence into this area, with the selection of the German Prince William of Wied to be the ruler in 1914. Although he did not take up his throne due to the onset of World War I in 1914, the Order of the Black Eagle, in five classes, and two merit medals, as well as a medal intended to commemorate the accession of the Prince were established. These items are certainly scarce if not rare.

Phase II begins in the 1920's when a tribal chief named Ahmed ben Zoghu proclaimed himself King Zog, and achieved an uneasy control of the country. He established the Order of Scanderbeg (an Albanian hero), and the Order of Fidelity (sometimes referred to as the Order of BESA from the initials on the badge.) The relative scarcity or rarity is hard to know as Zog on occasion was supposed to have sold some as a "revenue raising" enterprise.

Phase III takes in the Italian occupation of 1939-44. The Orders were issued were continued but in a modified form. Presumably, they were made in Italy.

While some copies may exist it they are not likely to be a problem for collectors.

The Orders of Albania were: the Black Eagle; Scanderbeg; Fidelity (sometimes referred to as the Order of BESA because of those initials on the obverse of the badge); and the Order of Bravery.

AUSTRIA
Holy Roman Empire (Austria) till 1806; Austrian Empire 1806-1867; Austro-Hungarian Empire (also Austria-Hungary) 1867-1918; Austrian Republic 1918-1938; Annexed Territory of the III Reich 1938-1945; Austrian Republic 1945.

As one of the countries that was among the first to grant Orders, Medals and Decorations, Austria provides many opportunities to the collector for enjoyment. Since this country's awards are so varied it is possible to form a collection around some of the themes mentioned earlier in Chapter I.

The Orders of "Austria", the generic title for the country for all time periods, have always presented a handsome appearance. This applies even to those established and awarded after World War II, in contrast to those of many other countries for the same time period.

However, it is the Austrian Orders up to 1918 which present the most problem for the collector. It is reasonable to state that all Austrian Orders up to 1918 should, or must be hallmarked in some way. The hallmark may take the form of a number to indicate gold content, such as 750 which equals 18 carat gold; or the manufacturer's (jewelers') name; or combination of same; or an asterisk to indicate bronze/gilt during World War I, sometimes with the manufacturer's name also. These marks appear mainly on the ribbon suspension rings, but also in some other places, depending on the particular Order. Thus, an unmarked badge of an Order should be regarded as a copy, restrike, or fake. The Maria Theresa Order was issued in gold. Silver/gilt insignia should be regarded with suspicion.

Another important feature of Austrian Orders is that suspension rings should be fused closed so that they cannot be opened. A suspension ring that can be opened is to be regarded as evidence of a copy or at least a replaced ring.

Bravery medals should have the name of the designer under the reigning monarch's bust on the obverse. During World War I there were examples in "pot metal" which do not have the designer's name. Some of these may be post World War I manufacture. There are gilt bronze copies of the Emperor Charles "gold" bravery medal, marked on the rim at the 1 o'clock position with the word UNECHT, meaning- not genuine. While there are genuine gold issues of the Franz Joseph bravery medal, the World War I issues tend to be bronze/gilt.

A distinctive features of Austrian awards worn on the chest is the triangular shaped ribbon. This is both a matter of interest as well as frustration to the collector, because they are not easy to replace when worn, or when missing. Curiously, this ribbon style was adopted for the Japanese Order of the Sacred Treasure IV-VIII classes, as well as for the awards of Bulgaria, Montenegro, Serbia, and Yugoslavia.

The collector may see a number of jewelers' marks on Austrian Orders. Among the most common are Karl Fischmeister, Vinc Mayer, Rothe & Neffe, and Scheid, for the Imperial period. Anton Reitterer is the maker of Austrian Republic Orders after World War II.

The Austrian Imperial Orders, and the Military Merit Cross, had a unique feature in regard to how they were worn on active service. There existed a device known as the "kleine dekoration"-literally "small decoration." A miniature badge of a higher grade of an Order would be worn on the ribbon of the lowest class. This allowed high ranking officers to show off their awards without having a massive display of breast stars, sashes, and neck badges. Thus, the recipient of the I Class of the Military Merit Cross, could/would wear a miniature badge on the III Class breast badge, instead of wearing a massive breast cross. Similarly for the Orders of Maria Theresa, Leopold, Iron Crown and Franz Joseph.

It was intended that the various bravery medals would be for enlisted men, while officers would get the Maria Theresa Order, and the Military Merit Cross. However, Emperor Charles in 1917 allowed the large Silver Bravery Medal, and the Gold Bravery Medal to be awarded to officers with the distinct of having a large "K" for Karl (Charles) on the ribbon. It is possible that some of the "K's" have been copied. Caution is in order.

The Orders of Austria up to 1918 were: the Golden Fleece (see also Spain); Maria Theresa (military); Leopold; the Iron Crown; Franz Joseph; Starry Cross (ladies); Elizabeth (ladies); Elizabeth Theresa (ladies).

For the Republic 1922-1938 there was the Honor Decoration for Merit 1922; later known as the Austrian Merit Order 1934-1938, with the insignia substantially the same.

BELGIUM
Province of various states until 1830; Kingdom since 1830.

The Orders, Medals and Decorations of Belgium are many and varied in their scope. They fall into two main categories, those of Belgium proper, and those of the Belgian colonial possession, the Belgian Congo (also known as the Independent State of the Congo when under the personal control of King Leopold II.) The awards of Belgium can be subdivided into two categories. In 1951 all Belgian awards which had the national motto "L'Union Fait la Force" (in unity there is strength) in French were converted into bilingual (French and Flemish) ones to reflect the continuing struggle of the nation's linguistic destiny. Although some earlier items were bilingual, such as the World War I Commemorative Medal, most had their inscription in French only.

Therefore, with Orders of Leopold, and Leopold II, and their attendant merit medals, there are two distinct types of awards to collect.

This country has been very generous, or prolific depending on your point of view, in its awards for both the military and civil sections of the population. Belgium's involvement in World Wars I and II saw a corresponding medallic flowering, compared to the much more restrained output of Great Britain and the United States.

Belgian awards are not difficult to come by because of the circumstances of their award. There are commercial establishments which sell Orders, Medals and Decorations, like any other commodity.

When one is granted a Belgian award, the recipient goes with the award document to such an establishment and has to buy it! However, members of the general public can buy these same items also.

Among the well known Belgian jewelers are Fisch, Heremans, and Wolfers. The current Court Jeweler is P. De Greef, and that name will be seen inside the cases of Belgian awards since World War II.

Happily for the collector the commercial manufacture of Belgian awards has meant that there is little fear of being stuck with copies. It is possible to assemble an impressive collection with much less cost than with other countries' material.

The Orders of Belgium include: Leopold; Leopold II; Crown; Lion of the Congo; Star of Africa.

BOXER REBELLION
China 1900-1901.

By the end of the 19th century, large parts of China, particularly the coastal areas and larger rivers had come under the "protection" or rather the control of foreign powers. All the great European powers, as well as the United States, and Japan, looked to China as a vast market for their manufactured goods, and investments.

The growth of foreign influence in China was due in part to ambitious and aggressive behavior of missionaries, merchants, as well as imperialist designs of government and military figures overseas. However, the continuing weakness of the Chinese governments and rulers was a substantial factor promoting the above. The appearance of anti-foreign movements therefore was not at all surprising.

One group in particular, the Society of Righteous Harmonious Fists, popularly known as the "Boxers" gained a great deal of support in its antagonism against foreign influence as exemplified by the Christian missionaries, who they believed were undermining traditional Chinese cultural values, and by outside powers who they believed were trying to take control of large chunks of the country.

The Imperial Chinese Government covertly encouraged the "Boxers" in their anti-foreignism, which ultimately led to armed rebellion against the foreign powers in 1900. The foreign diplomatic enclave in Peking, the capital, was attacked and besieged, and foreign diplomats, merchants, and missionaries were attacked and killed.

The various powers involved in Chinese commerce, or territorial land grabbing decided to send expeditionary forces to China to reassert their power and influence.

Medallically speaking, all of this resulted in the issuance of a variety of medals to commemorate this campaign.

Medals were issued by France; Germany-bronze for combatants, steel for non-combatants; Great Britain-silver for combatants, bronze for non-combatants, and a separate silver medal for the Merchant Marine; Italy-a medal reverse dated 1900-1902, and an undated one for the subsequent occupation forces; Japan; Russia-silver for officers, bronze for enlisted men; and the United States of America-with separate medals for the Army, Navy and Marine Corps.

The French medal had a silver bar 1900 CHINE 1901 slipped over the ribbon. The German combat medal had several campaign bars fixed onto the ribbon. The British medal had bars Relief of Pekin, Taku Forts, and Defense of Legations fixed to the medal, depending on the entitlement of the recipient. The British medals were officially named. The medal with bar for Defense of Legations is exceedingly rare, and especially prized by collectors. The United States medals were officially numbered, and medals to the Marine Corps are especially sought after.

While Austria-Hungary was a participant in the expedition it did not issue a special medal for this campaign. Instead, its men received the General Campaign Medal of 1873.

BRAZIL
Empire till 1889; Federal Republic.

The awards of this country fall into two phases. The first is from the monarchy which existed for most of the 19th century. The second stems from the republic.

Thus, the Order of the Southern Cross has two distinct types, with the first being rare. The Brazilian Empire also produced one of the most beautiful orders, namely, that of the Order of the Rose. Rare in all classes, it is a stunning tribute to the jeweler's art.

The Orders, Decorations, and Medals of this country are colorful, but their appearance varies considerably. Some of the medals from the 19th century Indian wars are rare, but do not find much favor with collectors outside of the country.

As a result of Brazil declaring war against Germany in both world conflicts there are for the collector a series of awards available.

For World War I, there is the War Cross, which is rare, and the Victory Medal in several variations. Copies exist of both these items.

For World War II there are the Naval Cross, the Distinguished Service Medal, the Naval War Service Medal, the Medal for Naval Force of the South, Medal for Naval Force of the Northeast, the Army War Medal, Brazilian Expeditionary Force Cross, the South Atlantic Campaign Medal, the Blood of Brazil Medal (a medal for wounds.)

The principal jeweler in this country is La Royale. This company has made insignia of Orders of a number of South American countries.

108

The Orders of the Brazilian Empire were: the Rose; Pedro I; the Southern Cross (type I).

The Orders of the Brazilian Republic are: the Southern Cross (type II); Naval Merit; Military Merit; Aeronautical Merit.

BULGARIA
Principality after 1878; Kingdom 1908-1944; People's Republic.

The awards of this country are many, varied, and very colorful. They show the influences of several foreign countries. As Bulgaria was established largely as a result of Russian power it is not surprising that early items were made in Russia, or that the Bravery Crosses for enlisted men were based deliberately on the Russian St George Cross. For example, 1st and 2nd Classes in gilt; 3rd and 4th classes silvered, with bow ribbons on the 1st and 3rd classes.

However, other countries' influences can be seen as well. German influence is characterized by the profusion of classes, and types of Orders. French influence is shown by the use of rosettes on the IV Class (Officer) insignia, and finally, Austrian influence by the triangular or trifold ribbon used on all Bulgarian breast awards. Most Orders, except for some very early ones, were Austrian made, and bore a princely crown from 1879-1908; thereafter an unusual royal crown.

The Bulgarian language is very similar to Russian, which results in some confusion for the collector.

The Orders of Bulgaria under the Kingdom included: the Military Order for Bravery; the Order of Saint Alexander, the Order of Merit, the Civil Merit Order, the Military Merit Order, the Order of Sts Cyril and Methodius, and the Red Cross Order.

CZECHOSLOVAKIA
(Includes Slovakia)
Former territory of the Austrian empire; republic since 1918.

The Orders, Medals and Decorations of this country reflect the country's heritage. Thus, common to its awards are the lion, and linden leaves, which both adorn a number of items.

The Order of the White Lion is distinctive and handsome. The high quality of its manufacture reflects great credit on the jeweler Karnet & Kysely. This Order was continued under the Communist regime, except that the Lion was uncrowned.

Czechoslovakia issued decorations and medals for both the World Wars, as well as commemorating its involvement in the Russian Civil War 1918-1919. The World War I Victory Medal appears in several variations.

The Orders include: Order of the White Lion, the Order of the Falcon (Sokol), the Order of Charles IV (sometimes referred to as the Decoration for the National Guard), Military Order of the White Lion, the Order of Jan Ziska, and the Military Order for Liberty.

DENMARK
Kingdom since the Middle Ages.

This country is one of the oldest in Europe in issuing Orders, going back to the Order of the Elephant. This Order is extremely rare, as besides being sparingly awarded it must be returned on the death of the recipient.

The Other Danish Order, the Dannebrog is an excellent example of the jeweler's art. Most of the badges are of gold,, and fine quality enamel. Since the cipher on the badges changes for each succeeding monarch it is possible, at least in theory, to assemble a collection based on this one Order. I say "in theory" since many pieces of this Order have been returned also. Presumably , those insignia that are on the market have been awarded to foreign recipients.

The premier jeweler to the Danish royal house has been the firm of A. Michelsen since 1848. The company hallmark is A.M.

ESTONIA
Province of Russia till 1918; republic 1919-1940. Forcibly incorporated into the U.S.S.R in 1940. Became independent again after the collapse of the Soviet Union in 1991.

The awards of this country exist in two phases. The first being from 1919-1940, after independence from Russia. The second, after the breakup of the U.S.S.R., and the re-emergence of an independent nation.

The remarks herein apply to phase one. The Estonian awards were of a high quality, with insignia being made by Roman Tavast. The awards of this country are rare on two accounts. Firstly, because this small country gave them out sparingly. Secondly. because much material either disappeared or was destroyed after the Soviet occupation of 1940.

Undoubtedly, there will be a mix of new and old in the awards system of this country. However, little of this material is likely to come on the market for collectors in the near future.

The Orders of this country include: the Order of the Cross of Liberty; the Order of the Coat of Arms of Estonia, the Order of the White Star, the Order of the Cross of the Eagle, and the Red Cross Order (a stunning example of the jeweler's art.)

FINLAND
Part of Sweden till 1809; Grand Duchy of the Russian Empire till 1918; republic since 1918.

Finland was one of the successor states of the Russian Empire. As such this country's awards carried on the Russian tradition of quality and appearance quite successfully. The national symbols of the Lion and the Rose are prevalent in their appearance. The Liberty Cross Order, however, is Germanic in its complexity of having so many classes, with and without swords.

The pre-World War II badges of the White Rose Order were silver/gilt and enamel. Post-war insignia appear to be bronze/gilt and enamel. Several jewelers have made Finnish Orders etc, but the most common is A. Tillander. Several hallmarks have been used with A.T. appearing frequently.

The Orders of this country include: Mannerheim Cross of the Liberty Cross Order, Order of the Liberty Cross, Order of the White Rose, Order of the Lion of Finland, Olympic Merit Order, Sports Merit Order, and the Order of the Holy Lamb.

Copies do not appear to be problem with this country's awards.

FRANCE
Kingdom till 1792; 1st Republic till 1802; 1st Empire 1802-1814; 1815; Kingdom 1814-1848; 2nd Republic 1848-1851; 2nd Empire 1851-1870; republic since 1871.

The concept of an award system belongs to France as a result of the Napoleonic period. The Emperor was the first to consider a deliberate program of making awards to men in the armed forces, as well as in civilian life, for merit, bravery and service to the state. The establishment of the Legion of Honor was the consequence.

There had been Orders in pre-revolutionary times, but they were severely restricted in their award based on social class. The Legion of Honor was the first of its kind for award on a "democratic" basis.

In later years this country would develop a very complex system of awards, wherein every department of government would have its own award system, with a three class Order, Commander, Officer and Knight.

The involvement of France in world affairs led to the creation of campaign medals commemorating activities from Mexico in 1862 to South East Asia in 1954. For a host of small campaigns a Colonial Service Medal with a multitude of bars or clasps was founded. The earliest bars for the latter were clip-on slipover. Later they were just stamped pieces of metal to be slipped over the medal ribbon.

The Legion of Honor as France's premier award may be seen in many guises, from 1804 to the present, with at least twelve distinct variations. For some reason the white enamel was not of a high quality. To find one of these items without chipping is something of an achievement.

The Médaille Militaire (Military Medal), an award for bravery, also has gone through several phases, with the originals bearing the head of Napoleon III.

The second phase had on the obverse the head of Marianne, of Republican France, and the date 1870 for the Third Republic, replaced by one star for the Fourth Republic, and followed by three stars for the Fifth Republic. The quality of this decoration has varied considerably.

In the United States many collectors are familiar with one item in particular, the Croix de Guerre (War Cross), because a number of the U.S. military were awarded it, particularly during World War I.

The Orders of France include: Legion of Honor, Order of the Holy Ghost, Order of St Michael, Military Order of St Louis, Military Merit Order, Order of the Reunion, Order of the Three Golden Fleece, Order of the Academic Palmes, Order of Liberation, Orders of Merit, namely, Agricultural, Maritime, Social, Public Health, Commercial, Artisan, Tourist, Combattent, Postal, National Economy, Sporting, Labor, Military, Civil, Arts and Letters, Saharan, and the National Order of Merit.

French Colonial Orders include: Black Star of Benin, Star of Anjouan, Nichan-El-Anouar, Dragon of Annam, Royal Order of Cambodia, and the Million Elephants and White Parasol of Laos.

GERMANY
States till 1871; Empire till 1918; Republic 1918-1933; III Reich 1933-1945; allied occupation 1945-1951; Federal Republic 1951.

No country offers more opportunities and pitfalls in collecting than Germany. The many states of Germany before unification, and after it, provide a multiplicity of awards to obtain. The complexity of some them requires much study in this field.. The Military Merit Order of Bavaria, and its attendant Military Merit Crosses, and the Peter Frederick Louis Order of Oldenberg are just two examples that come to mind. The vast array of awards of the III Reich is also of great collector interest.

Unfortunately, for the collector there is also the problem of fakes and/or copies. One of the most popular German (Prussian) awards is the Pour Le Mérite (often referred to as the "Blue Max"). The copies of this award are legendary, and of great variation in quality.

Other than Great Britain, this country's awards offer the most flexibility for collecting. One can concentrate on a particular state. One can collect long service awards from all the states. One can collect from a time period, such as the Napoleonic Wars or World War I.

Because many of the component states of the German Empire issued Orders, Medals, and Decorations at one time or another, there are many private jewelers who made the awards, in lieu of the official state mints which struck coins, although the Konigl. Munzamt (Royal Mint) of Stuttgart did make various insignia of the Wurttemberg Orders.

Among the famous makers were Godet of Berlin, known to have made awards of most of the German states, the III Reich (German Eagle Order) as well as insignia for other countries; Gerbruder Hemmerle, the Royal Bavarian Orders; C.E. Juncker, especially known for many badges of the III Reich; Knauer, for the Peter Frederick Louis Order of Oldenberg; Wagner, maker of Prussian Orders. This is only a small sampling of the various jewelers. For more detailed information consult Jeffrey Jacob **COURT JEWELERS OF THE WORLD**.

The Orders of Germany will be listed by States.

ANHALT:
Albert the Bear, Merit Order for Arts and Science.

BADEN:
Military Karl-Friedrich Order, Zahringen Lion, Berthold I.

BAVARIA:
St Hubert, St George, House and Knightly Order of St Michael, Military Order of Max Joseph, Bavarian Crown, Royal Order of St Michael, Military Merit Order, Arts and Science, Ludwig, Military Sanitary, Elizabeth, Theresia, St Anne.

BRUNSWICK:
Henry the Lion, Arts and Science.

FRANKFURT:
Concordia.

HANNOVER:
St George, Guelphic Order (see also Great Britain), Ernst-August.

HESSE-DARMSTADT:
Golden Lion, Ludwig, Philip the Brave, Star of Brabant.

HESSE-KASSEL:
Golden Lion, Wilhelm, Military Virtue, Iron Helmet.

HOHENLOHE:
Phoenix.

HOHENZOLLERN:
House Order (see also Prussia and Rumania), Bene-Merenti.

ISENBERG-BIRSTEIN:
House Order.

LIPPE-DETMOLD:
Honor Cross, Leopold, Bertha, Arts and Science (Lippe Rose).

MECKLENBERG-SCHWERIN:
Wendish Crown, Griffin.

MECKLENBERG-STRELITZ:
Wendish Crown.
NASSAU:
Golden Lion, Adolph of Nassau.
OLDENBURG:
Peter Frederick Louis.
PRUSSIA:
Black Eagle, Merit Order of the Prussian Crown, Pour le Mérite (civil and military), Red Eagle, Crown, Hohenzollern (see also Hohenzollern and Rumania), Johanniter, Louise, Iron Cross.
REUSS:
Honor Cross.
SAXONY:
Rue Crown, St Henry, Civil Merit, Albert, Maria Anna.
SAXE-WEIMAR:
White Falcon.
SAXE-COBURG-SAALFELD:
St Joachim.
SAXON-DUCHIES:
Saxe-Ernestine House Order.
SCHAUMBURG-LIPPE:
House Order, Arts and Science.
SCHLESWIG-HOLSTEIN:
St Anne.
SCHWARZBURG (Rudolstadt & Sonderhausen):
Honor Cross, Merit.
THURN AND TAXIS:
Perfect Amity.
WALDECK:
Merit.
WESTPHALIA:
Westphalian Crown.
WUERTEMBERG:
St Hubert, Crown, Civil Merit, Carl Military Order, Military Merit, Friedrich, and Olga.
THIRD REICH:
German Eagle Order, National Prize for Arts and Science, German Red Cross, Social Welfare Decoration, and the Iron Cross.
FEDERAL REPUBLIC:
Merit.

GREAT BRITAIN
Kingdom of England and Scotland 1603-1707; Great Britain 1707-1801; United Kingdom of Great Britain and Ireland till 1921; United Kingdom of Great Britain and N. Ireland to date.

The Orders, Medals and decorations of this country are richly varied in their complexity. The quality of workmanship has been maintained right up to the present, although perhaps the design has not.

For many collectors the British Campaign Medals are the most fascinating and rewarding area to collect. Since most are named, and records quite complete, it is possible to research recipients' careers.

The history of the British Empire is written its campaign medals. Africa alone provided the basis for sixty campaign awards; some commemorated by specific medals, and others by bars or clasps to general service medals. General service medals were a basic award for an area to which bars (clasps) were affixed on to the medal to indicate a specific conflict. The Indian Empire, for example, is commemorated by the Order of the Star of India, the Order of the Indian Empire, the Order of the Crown of India, the Army of India Medal 1799-1826, the India General Service Medal 1854-1895, the India General Service Medal 1895-1902, the India General Service Medal 1908-1935, and the India General Service Medal 1936-1939.

The Orders of Great Britain have been made variously by the Royal Mint, and by private jewelers. Items made by the Royal Mint are not hallmarked, because the established gold and silver standards are automatically presumed to be in use by that body. However, privately made insignia, and/or medals are hallmarked with the city of manufacture, the date, and the silver or gold standard. Some of the important private jewelers have been: Collingwood, Elkington & Co., Garrard, Gaunt & Son, Hancock (makers of the Victoria Cross), and Spink & Son Ltd.

The awards of this country have been made to high standards. Fakes and copies are less of a problem than for those of some other countries. However, since the development of laser manufacturing techniques more problems are likely to arise. Obviously, it is easier to fake unnamed decorations, and medals, since the impressing or engraving style might be complicated to duplicate.

Great Britain, and to some extent other Commonwealth countries have followed the practice of allowing letters to appear after the name of a recipient (postnomial letters) to indicate an award. For the convenience of the collector they are listed below in alphabetical order, not the order of precedence. Some of these may still be in use by other Commonwealth countries, but they are intended to provide information for the collector of British items.

A.F.C.-AIR FORCE CROSS
A.F.M.-AIR FORCE MEDAL
A.M.-ALBERT MEDAL
A.R.R.C.-ASSOCIATE OF THE ROYAL RED CROSS

B.E.M.-BRITISH EMPIRE MEDAL
B.G.M.-BURMA GALLANTRY MEDAL

C.B.-COMPANION OF THE ORDER OF THE BATH
C.B.E.-COMMANDER OF THE ORDER OF THE BRITISH EMPIRE
C.G.M.-CONSPICUOUS GALLANTRY MEDAL
C.H.-COMPANION OF HONOUR
C.I.E.-COMPANION OF THE ORDER OF THE INDIAN EMPIRE
C.M.G.-COMPANION OF THE ORDER OF STS MICHAEL AND GEORGE
C.S.C.-CONSPICUOUS SERVICE CROSS
C.St.J.-COMMANDER OF THE ORDER OF ST JOHN OF JERUSALEM
C.V.O.-COMMANDER OF THE ROYAL VICTORIAN ORDER

D.B.E.-DAME COMMANDER OF THE ORDER OF THE BRITISH EMPIRE
D.C.B.-DAME COMMANDER OF THE ORDER OF THE BATH
D.C.M.-DISTINGUISHED CONDUCT MEDAL
D.C.V.O.-DAME COMMANDER OF THE ROYAL VICTORIAN ORDER
D.F.C.-DISTINGUISHED FLYING CROSS
D.F.M.-DISTINGUISHED FLYING MEDAL
D.S.C.-DISTINGUISHED SERVICE CROSS
D.S.M.-DISTINGUISHED SERVICE MEDAL
D.S.O.-DISTINGUISHED SERVICE ORDER
D.St.J.-DAME OF THE ORDER OF ST JOHN OF JERUSALEM

E.D.-EFFICIENCY DECORATION
E.G.M.-EMPIRE GALLANTRY MEDAL
E.M.-EDWARD MEDAL
E.R.D.-EMERGENCY RESERVE DECORATION

G.B.E.-KNIGHT/DAME GRAND CROSS OF THE ORDER OF THE BRITISH EMPIRE
G.C.-GEORGE CROSS
G.C.B.-KNIGHT GRAND CROSS OF THE BATH
G.C.H.-KNIGHT GRAND CROSS OF THE HANOVERIAN ORDER-till 1837

G.C.I.E.-KNIGHT GRAND COMMANDER OF THE ORDER OF THE INDIAN EMPIRE

G.C.M.G.-KNIGHT GRAND CROSS OF THE ORDER OF STS MICHAEL AND GEORGE

G.C.S.I.-KNIGHT GRAND COMMANDER OF THE ORDER OF THE STAR OF INDIA

G.C.St.J.-BAILIFF/DAME GRAND CROSS OF THE ORDER OF ST JOHN OF JERUSALEM

G.C.V.O.-KNIGHT/DAME GRAND CROSS OF THE ROYAL VICTORIAN ORDER

G.M.-GEORGE MEDAL

I.D.S.M.-INDIAN DISTINGUISHED SERVICE MEDAL

I.O.M.-INDIAN ORDER OF MERIT

I.S.O.-IMPERIAL SERVICE ORDER

K.B.-KNIGHT OF THE ORDER OF THE BATH-pre 1815

K.B.E-KNIGHT COMMANDER OF THE ORDER OF THE BRITISH EMPIRE

K.C.B.-KNIGHT COMMANDER OF THE ORDER OF THE BATH

K.C.H.-KNIGHT COMMANDER OF THE HANOVERIAN ORDER

K.C.I.E.-KNIGHT COMMANDER OF THE ORDER OF THE INDIAN EMPIRE

K.C.M.G.-KNIGHT COMMANDER OF THE ORDER OF STS MICHAEL AND GEORGE

K.C.S.I.-KNIGHT COMMANDER OF THE ORDER OF THE STAR OF INDIA

K.G.-KNIGHT OF THE ORDER OF THE GARTER

K.H.-KNIGHT OF THE HANOVERIAN ORDER

K.P.-KNIGHT OF THE ORDER OF ST PATRICK

K.P.M.-KING'S POLICE MEDAL

K.St.J.-KNIGHT OF THE ORDER OF ST JOHN OF JERUSALEM

K.T.-KNIGHT OF THE ORDER OF THE THISTLE

L.V.O.-LIEUTENANT OF THE ROYAL VICTORIAN ORDER

M.B.E.-MEMBER OF THE ORDER OF THE ORDER OF THE BRITISH EMPIRE

M.C.-MILITARY CROSS

M.M.-MILITARY MEDAL

M.S.M.-MERITORIOUS SERVICE MEDAL

M.V.O.-MEMBER OF THE ROYAL VICTORIAN ORDER

O.B.-ORDER OF BURMA
O.B.E-OFFICER OF THE ORDER OF THE BRITISH EMPIRE
O.B.I.-ORDER OF BRITISH INDIA
O.M.-ORDER OF MERIT
O.St.J.-SERVING OFFICER OF THE ORDER OF ST JOHN OF
JERUSALEM

Q.F.M.-QUEEN'S FIRE MEDAL
Q.G.M.-QUEEN'S GALLANTRY MEDAL
Q.P.M.-QUEEN'S POLICE MEDAL

R.D.-RESERVE DECORATION
R.R.C.-ROYAL RED CROSS
R.V.M.-ROYAL VICTORIAN MEDAL

S.B.St.J.-SERVING BROTHER OF THE ORDER OF ST JOHN OF
JERUSALEM
S.G.M.-SEA GALLANTRY MEDAL
S.S.St.J.-SERVING SISTER OF THE ORDER OF ST JOHN OF
JERUSALEM

T.D.-TERRITORIAL DECORATION

V.C.-VICTORIA CROSS
V.D.-VOLUNTEER DECORATION
V.R.D.-VOLUNTEER RESERVE DECORATION

Since most of the awards of this country are named it was thought to
be useful to provide a comprehensive listing of abbreviations to be found
on them. This will include ranks, and units.

RANKS
Army
Bmbdr-Bombardier; Brig-Brigadier; Brig Gen-Brigadier General; Col-
Colonel; Con.-Conductor; Cpl-Corporal; CQMS-Company Quartermaster
Sergeant; CSM-Company Sergeant Major; Fus.-Fusilier; Farr Sjt-Farrier
Serjeant; L/Cpl-Lance Corporal; Lt & Lieut-Lieutenant; Lieut Col-
Lieutenant Colonel; Lt or Lieut Gen-Lieutenant General; Mus.-Musician;
Pte-Private; RSM-Regimental Sergeant Major; Sgt-Sergeant; Sjt-Serjeant;
RQMS-Regimental Quartermaster Sergeant; Sig.-Signalman; Tptr-
Trumpeter; WOI-Warrant Officer I Class (=Regimental Sergeant Major);
WOII-Warrant Officer Class II (=Company Sergeant Major).

British Indian Army
Spellings of some of the ranks may vary by period, that is by the inscription on 19th and 20th century medals.

Ranks
Officers
Subadar-Major-senior infantry officer
Subadar-1st ranking company infantry officer.
Jemedar-2nd ranking company infantry officer.
Risaldar-Major-senior cavalry officer.
Risaldar-commanding troop of cavalry.

Enlisted Men
Duffadar=Cavalry Sergeant
Duffadar-Major=Regimental Sergeant Major of Cavalry
Quartermaster Duffadar=Regimental Quartermaster Sergeant of Cavalry.
Havildar=Infantry Sergeant.
Havildar-Major=Regimental Sergeant Major of Infantry.
Quartermaster Havildar=Regimental Quartermaster Sergeant of Infantry.
Golundauze=Artilleryman.
Lascar=Low ranking artilleryman.
Naik=Corporal of Infantry.
Sepoy=Infantry Private (usually Sep. on medals.)
Sowar=Cavalry Private.
Tindal=Artillery NCO commanding Lascars.

Occupations found on medals to Indian Units
BHISTI-Water Carrier (Gunga Din was one of these).
DHOBI-Washerman.
DHOOLIE-BEARER (various spellings)-Stretcher bearer.
KHIDMATGAR-Table servant.
KOTWAL-Head man of followers.
LANGRI-Cook.
MEHTA-Sweeper.
NALBUND-Farrier or blacksmith.
SYCE-Groom.

SOME REGIMENTAL AND UNIT ABBREVIATIONS OF THE BRITISH ARMY

A & SH-Argyll & Sutherland Highlanders; AAC-Army Air Corps; ACC-Army Catering Corps; ASC-Army Service Corps
BW-Black Watch

DG-Dragoon Guards; DLI-Durham Light Infantry; DWR-Duke of Wellington's Regiment;

Gren Gds-Grenadier Guards; GR-Gurkha Regiment; GTR-Gurkha Transport Regiment

H (with number before it e.g. 15th/19th)-Hussars; HAC-Honorable Artillery; HLI-Highland Light Infantry

IG-Irish Guards; IMD-Indian Medical Department; IY & Imp Yeo-Imperial Yeomanry

KOSB-Kings Own Scottish Borderers; KOYLI-Kings Own Yorkshire Light Infantry; KRRC-Kings Royal Rifle Corps; KSLI-Kings Own Shropshire Light Infantry;

L (with number before it e.g. 17th/21st)-Lancers; LG-Life Guards

Ox & Bucks-Oxford and Buckingham Light Infantry

NI-Native Infantry

QARANC-Queen Alexandra's Royal Army Nursing Corps; QDG-Queens Dragoon Guards;

RA-Royal Artillery; RAC-Royal Armoured Corps; RAChD-Royal Army Chaplain's Department; RADC-Royal Army Dental Corps; RAEC-Royal Army Educational Corps; RAMC-Royal Army Medical Corps; RAOC-Royal Army Ordnance Corps; RAPC-Royal Army Pay Corps; RASC-Royal Army Service Corps; RAVC-Royal Army Veterinary Corps; RB-Rifle Brigade; RE-Royal Engineers; REME-Royal Electrical and Mechanical Engineers; RF-Royal Fusiliers; RFA-Royal Field Artillery; RGJ-Royal Green Jackets; RHA-Royal Horse Artillery; RH-Royal Highlanders (Black Watch); RHG-Royal Horse Guards; RIF-Royal Irish Fusiliers; RIR-Royal Irish Rifles; RMP-Royal Military Police; RNB Dragoons-Royal North British Dragoons (Royal Scots Greys); RPC-Royal Pioneer Corps; RS-Royal Scots; RTR-Royal Tank Regiment; RWK-Royal West Kent

SAS-Special Air Service; SG-Scots Guards

UDR-Ulster Defense Regiment

WG-Welsh Guards

Royal Navy-R.N.

Ranks and Rates (Occupations)

AB-Able Seaman; Adm-Admiral; Cdr-Commander; Cox'n-Coxswain; CPO-Chief Petty Officer; ERA-Engineroom Artificer; L/Cdr-LT Commander; LS-Leading Seaman; L/Sto-Leading Stoker; MAA-Master-at-Arms; OS-Ordinary Seaman; PO-Petty Officer; RAdm-Rear Admiral; SBA-Sick Berth Attendant; Sto-Stoker; VAdm-Vice Admiral; WRO Servt-Ward Room Officers' Servant; Yeo-Yeoman of...;

Royal Air Force-R.A.F.
Ranks
AM-Air Marshal; ACM-Air Chief Marshal; AVM-Air Vice Marshal; F/L-Flight Lieutenant; F/O-Flying Officer; FSgt-Flight Sergeant; GC-Group Captain; LAC-Leading Aircraftman; P/O-Pilot Officer; Sqn Ldr-Squadron Leader; W/Cdr-Wing Commander.

The Orders of this country include: the Garter, the Thistle, St Patrick (obsolete), the Bath (in two divisions military and civil), Sts Michael and George, Guelphic (1815-1837, see also German state of Hannover), the Star of India (obsolete), the Indian Empire (obsolete) Victoria and Albert, the Crown of India (obsolete), Merit (in two types civil, and military with swords the only British Order to have such), Companion of Honour, the Royal Victorian Order, British Empire, St John, and the Royal Family Orders.

GREECE
Independent from Turkey in 1829; with brief exceptions was a monarchy till the 1970's, now a republic.

The Orders, Medals, and Decorations of this country reflect its turbulent history in modern times. Its first awards involve the German State of Bavaria, one of whose Princes became the first ruler of an independent Greece in the early 19th century. His replacement by a member of the Danish royal family saw a change in the country's award insignia. Later, there were republics, and consequently further changes.
Many of the Greek awards are stunning in appearance, especially the Order of the Redeemer. Some are also unprepossessing in appearance, especially some of the bravery awards of the armed forces.
Greece in common with many of the victorious nations issued a Victory Medal for World War I, with a unique suspension, not only for this medal series, but for all awards anywhere!
The Orders of this country include: the Redeemer, George I, the Phoenix (there are several types), Sts George and Constantine, Sts Olga and Sophia, and Good Deeds (or Charity).

HUNGARY
Part of the Austrian Empire till 1918, a titular monarchy from 1922-1944. Became a People's Republic until the downfall of the U.S.S.R.

The Orders, Medals and Decorations of this country (that is for the period 1922-1944) were directly descended from those of the awards of the

Austro-Hungarian Empire. They continued the distinctive trifold ribbon, the kleine dekoration, the Red Cross awards, and the "Signum Laudis" to name some.

The Order of St Stephen, which was always considered a Hungarian award, was continued to be allowed to be worn, but it is not clear whether additional insignia were awarded. Care should be taken with this order. Badges should be hallmarked on the suspension. Unmarked pieces, no matter how well made they are should be avoided, unless one likes buying copies.

As Hungary was allied to the III Reich during World War II there was an exchange of decorations etc between the two.

The Order of the Holy Crown was established during World War II, and is scarce to rare in all grades.

The World War I Commemorative Medal was awarded in combat form with swords on the obverse, and in non-combat form without the swords. The former is often seen in mounted German medal groups.

The Orders of this country include: St Stephen (originated under the Austrian Empire), Golden Spur, Vitez, Merit, Holy Crown, and the Honor Decoration of the Red Cross.

ICELAND
Colony of Denmark till 1944; Republic since 1944.

The only Order of this country is the Order of the Icelandic Falcon. When part of Denmark the insignia were made by Michelsen of Copenhagen. Since 1944 Kjartan Asmundsson of Reykyavik has been the maker. Thus, it has come in two types: 1.With crown suspension under the Danish Kingdom. 2.Without crown suspension under the Icelandic Republic.

Unmarked insignia have been made in France.

IRELAND
Became independent from Great Britain after World War I.

The Republic of Ireland, since gaining its independence from Great Britain, has been very circumspect in making awards to its people, military or civilian, with the exception of the War of Independence, for which three medals, the Easter Rising Medal, General Service Medal (Black and Tan) with and without combat bar. The "Black and Tan" medal is so-called after its ribbon half black/half tan, which commemorates the special British forces raised after World War I, which wore a combination uniform of police tunic (black), and army trousers (tan).

For World War II, there was the Emergency Service Medal 1939-1946, which was issued to a variety of units, designated on the reverse, with extra service bars on the ribbon. Some of these are very common, and some are rare. See identification section for further details.

Most other Irish awards are rare. Irish troops also qualified for various United Nations Service Medal, notably with the Cyprus ribbon.

ITALY
Became a unified kingdom in 1860. This lasted until the establishment of a republic in 1946.

The awards of this country are among the earliest in Europe, particularly those of the Duchy of Savoy, which became the nucleus of the Kingdom of Italy. The Order of the Annunciation (Annunziata) dates to 1360, and the Order of Sts Maurice and Lazarus to 1434. The Military Valor Medal (Al Valore Militare) of Piedmont-Sardinia, later of the Kingdom of Italy, dates to 1793.

As with the German Empire, there were independent states, which issued their own awards. However, in contradistinction to the German states, the unification of Italy saw the official abolition of the awards of the various Italian states, although some continued to be granted as personal awards of the previous reigning family. The problem exists with the Orders in that it may be very difficult to discern whether an item is pre-1860 (the date of Italian unification) or post-1860. Sometimes the quality of the workmanship or enameling is a clue.

Among the Italian states' awards one may find those of the Duchy of Lucca; the Duchy of Parma; the Kingdom of the Two Sicilies, also known as the Kingdom of Naples; the Grand Duchy of Tuscany; the Republic of Venice; the Duchy of Savoy which became in succession the Kingdom of Piedmont, the Kingdom of Piedmont-Sardinia, and finally the Kingdom of Italy, after the annexation and unification of formerly existing states in 1860-1870; the Papal States (Vatican).

For a short time in World War II (from 1943-1945), there emerged the Italian Social Republic, a fascist puppet state set up for Mussolini in Northern Italy. Genuine awards of this "state" are scarce to rare.

The awards of Italy are comparable to those of several countries, with orders, long service medals, gallantry awards, and various commemorative items.

Moreover, there is also a host of semi-official or unofficial unit medals issued by "armies", divisions, regiments, battalions and the like. Many of these were issued for the campaigns in East Africa leading to the conquest of Ethiopia in 1935.

There is an unusual feature in the suspension on most Italian medals. At the top of the medal there is a horizontal piece of medal with the ends turned inward at a roughly 45 degree angle and soldered to the medal rim. The ribbon goes through this. Anyone who has tried to ribbon an Italian medal with this suspension can testify to the frustration in trying to get it looking even and smart.

Italy in common with most of the countries involved in the Boxer Rebellion 1900-1901 issued a campaign medal. Reverse bears the word CINA 1900-1902. In Italian CINA is pronounced "CHEENA". Italy issued also another medal for the occupation after the suppression of the rebellion, identical to the previous one except that the date was omitted.

After World War I Italy in concert with the other victors issued the Victory Medal.

Since Italy was on opposite sides in World Wars I and II her decorations were awarded to recipients in many countries.

For the collector there is no real problem with copies, except for the awards of the Italian Social Republic. Having said this, the author must admit that in his early days he did get caught with a cast copy of the Victory Medal.

Some of the well-known jewelers of this country are Cravanzola, Gardino, Stefano Johnson (see also S. Johnson or S.J.), Tanfani and Bertarelli.

For the Kingdom of Italy the most common oldest logo seen on Orders is that of Cravanzola, which was succeeded by Gardino. Stefano Johnson is the current maker of the Republic's Orders, as well as the manufacturer of restrikes, reissues of earlier awards. Jeffrey Jacob in his **COURT JEWELERS OF THE WORLD** notes that the Orders of the pre-1860 were apparently unmarked. It appears that marked insignia of the various states would indicate post-1860 production. However, that cannot be regarded as the definitive statement on the matter.

Orders of the Former Italian States include:

DUCHY OF LUCCA 1805-1847
St George, and St Louis.
DUCHY OF MODENA 1452-1860
Eagle of Este.
DUCHY OF (BOURBON) PARMA 1545-1859
Constantine of St George, and St Louis (see also Lucca).
KINGDOM OF THE TWO SICILIES (NAPLES)
St Januarius (many variations), St Ferdinand, Royal Order of the Two Sicilies, St George of the Reunion, and Francis I.
GRAND DUCHY OF TUSCANY
St Stephen, St Joseph, Military Merit, and Civil Merit.

DUCHY OF SAVOY/KINGDOM OF PIEDMONT-SARDINIA/ KINGDOM OF ITALY

Annunciation (Annunziata), Sts Maurice and Lazarus, Military Savoy; Civil Savoy, Crown of Italy (see also the Iron Crown of Austria), Colonial Merit, and the Roman Eagle (copies are known).

Awards of the Kingdom of Italy generally had to be purchased by the recipient.

JAPAN

An empire. The modern Japanese state stems from the reign of the Emperor Meiji in the 1860's. Manchukuo was a Japanese puppet "empire" established in Manchuria from 1931-1945.

One of the results of Japan leaving its isolation in the mid-19th century was its adoption of an awards system for its noble and military classes. Since there was no tradition of knighthood in the Western sense, this country's awards were based on a simple system of merit.

The highest Order, the Chrysanthemum, was like that of the highest European Orders in that it was a one class award.

The Orders of this country were/are linked to emblems of its heritage, and so there was the Order of the Golden Kite (in seven classes), the Rising Sun (in eight classes), and the Sacred Treasure (in eight classes). For the fourth classes the French style rosette as a distinguishing feature was used, although not the designation of Officer. An even more curious thing is to be found with the ribbon of the fourth through eighth classes which is the Austrian style trifold ribbon, although with the typical Japanese hook and eye fastener on the reverse.

Unlike most other countries Japan did not issue specific medals for bravery, instead using the VI and VII classes of the Golden Kite Order. As part of the reforms intended to eliminate militarism from Japanese society the Golden Kite Order was abolished after World War II. Most of the awards of Japan were made by the Osaka Mint.

Orders of Japan include: Chrysanthemum, Grand Cordon of the Rising Sun, the Rising Sun, Golden Kite, Sacred Crown (for ladies, and rare in all classes), and the Sacred Treasure.

Orders of Manchukuo include: Illustrious Dragon, Auspicious Clouds, and the Pillars of State. Each of these are counterparts to Japanese Orders, and were abolished at the end of World War II.

LATVIA

Province of Russia till 1918; republic 1919-1940. Forcibly incorporated into the U.S.S.R in 1940. Became independent again after the collapse of the Soviet Union in 1991.

The collector of awards from this country must face the fact that all material is at least scarce, as much of it was issued in a very short period from 1919-1940. During the Soviet and German occupations a great deal was hidden or destroyed as a safety measure.

The most commonly seen Order is that of the Three Stars, which was frequently awarded to foreign diplomats.

The Orders of this country include: the Bearslayer, the Three Stars, Vesthardus, Recognition, and the Red Cross. W.F. Muller of Riga was the most prominent jeweler, especially noted for making the Order of the Three Stars.

There does not seem to be a problem with copies.

LITHUANIA

Province of Russia till 1918; republic 1919-1940. Forcibly incorporated into the U.S.S.R in 1940. Became independent again after the collapse of the Soviet Union in 1991.

As with to Estonia, and Latvia, this country became independent after World War I and the Russian Revolution/Civil War. Its period of independence lasted from 1919-1940, resuming after the collapse of the Soviet Union.

Its Orders include: Vytautus, Cross of Vytis, and Gedeminas. Only the last can be considered fairly common, as a number were awarded to foreign recipients.

There does not appear to be a problem with copies of this country's awards.

LUXEMBURG

Grand Duchy

The awards of this country fall into two categories. The ruling house of the German state of Nassau was directly connected with the ruling house of Luxemburg, so that the premier Order of the Golden Lion was also a Nassau Order. This Order in any class is very rare. The Order of Adolph of Nassau is likewise rare.

The Order of the Oaken Crown is quite often seen. One way to tell the age of the IV Class (Officer) is by the design. The earlier issues had an oak wreath between the arms, the later issues are without the wreath, but with a French style rosette between the arms.

The Order of Adolph shows the German influence of the swords between the arms, in its military version.

Although this country was occupied by Germany in both World Wars it only issued a volunteers' medal for the first. For World War II there was a Croix de Guerre, of which there are two versions. One is very similar to the Belgian Croix de Guerre, and another is a completely flat type. There was also a Military Medal, a Volunteers' Medal, and two awards for the Resistance.

Except for the Orders of the Oaken Crown, and National Merit this country's awards are seldom seen.

There does not seem to be problem of copies. It appears that most awards of this country were made in Holland and Germany before World War I, and in Holland and Belgium afterwards.

The Orders of Luxembourg include; Golden Lion, Adolph, Oaken Crown, and Merit.

MEXICO
Became independent from Spain in 1821; now a federal republic.

The Orders, Medals and Decorations of this country are quite complex. The best reference available appears to Frank Grove **THE MEDALS OF MEXICO-volume 3.**

There are several periods in which the awards can be divided, and the one apparently of most interest in the Maximilian period 1862-1867. The issue by Maximilian of Hapsburg, as "Emperor of Mexico" of several Orders and decorations has captured the imagination of collectors. The Order of Our Lady of Guadalupe was revived under this regime in both military and civil versions. Various medals were struck by the French, and bear the names of medallic designers of the time. See also the French Mexico medal.

The Order of the Aztec Eagle is currently Mexico's highest award, is scarce to rare in all grades, and is a fine example of the designer's art.

MONACO
Principality on the south coast of France.

The Orders of this tiny principality include Grimaldi, St Charles, and Cultural Merit. The inscription on the last indicates that it is from Monaco. The Orders are well made by the French jeweler Aubert. There is no problem with copies.

NETHERLANDS
This country emerged from the Napoleonic Wars to become a kingdom. A revolt in 1830 resulted in the creation of Belgium as a separate nation.

The Orders, Medals, and Decorations of this country are varied and colorful. As a onetime important power the awards of this country reflect its turbulent history. Its campaign medals go back to before the Napoleonic era.

127

The Netherlands, in common with other European countries, came to possess an overseas empire, principally in the S. Pacific, in what is now called Indonesia, previously the Dutch (or Netherlands) East Indies. This resulted in a number of campaign awards. For the most part, campaign action was commemorated with the issue of the Expedition Cross, to whose ribbon could be added a bar or bars to indicate specific campaigns. Some of these bars have been copied.

The Netherlands also issued a decoration for service in the Korean War. It was called the Cross for Right and Freedom, with the intention of using it for other situations, although never actually so employed. It can be found with one to three bars KOREA 1950, 2 KOREA 1950, and 3 KOREA 1950, the last being rare.

A major jeweler has been J. M. J. Van Wielik of The Hague, and Amsterdam.

The Orders of the Netherlands include: the Reunion (Kingdom of Holland), Royal Merit (Kingdom of Holland), William, Netherlands Lion, Orange-Nassau, and the Nassau House Order.

NORWAY
Became an independent kingdom in 1906.

Norway became independent of Sweden in 1906. Its Order of St Olav existed before that date. The medal for Heroic Deeds was established in 1885, and as a pre-independence medal is highly prized if to a Norwegian.

As a result of involvement in World War II this country issued several awards, most of which were for service in the resistance, or for service with allied forces. Norway also issued a medal for the Korean War, although it was involved only in a non-combat role.

The official jeweler is J.Tostrup of Oslo, pieces sometimes being marked with J.Tostrup or J.T.

PHILIPPINES
Colony of Spain until 1898, and then of the U.S.A. till 1946; independent republic 1946.

The awards of this country can be divided into two periods; under American control, and independent status; three if one includes the Spanish colonial service medals for this country.

Thus, the Medal for valor, which corresponds to the U.S. Medal of Honor, can be seen in the two types, first for the Commonwealth under U.S. control, and then the republic version. Several of the campaign medals have been issued in "Commonwealth of the Philippines" and Republic issues, with the earlier issues being of more collector interest, especially in the U.S.A.

128

The three most commonly seen Filipino medals in the U.S.A. are the Defense, Liberation, and Independence Medals. Since many U.S. servicemen qualified for these items, early issues are most sought after. There are many varieties of these three medals, some of which have been made in the U.S.A.; quality varies considerably.

Officially made pieces may be marked J.Tupaz Sr; J.Tupaz Jr; El Oro; or some combination of these.

Orders in their higher grades may come in a brown wooden case; medals and decorations come in a variety of colored cardboard boxes; some orange, some green, some gold and black, and some multicolored.

See also Spain for medals relating to the colonial period, and the United States of America for medals relating to rebellions which took place shortly after the American defeat of Spain in 1898.

The Orders of this country include: Sikatuna, and the Legion of Honor.

POLAND
Elective monarchy until 1795 when it was divided up by Prussia, Austria and Russia; republic in 1918 after the downfall of the Russian Empire.

The Orders, Medals and Decorations of this country have gone through as many contortions as has the political life of the country.

Awards exist from this country prior to the first partition in 1774. In 1795 the country was divided up between Prussia, Austria, and Russia. It was under the latter that some semblance of the awards system was continued.

The Emperor of Russia, as Tsar of Poland, continued to award the Order of the White Eagle, the Order of St Stanislaus, and the Order of Military Virtue (Virtuti Militari). Please note the previous statement is a simplification of the various changes taking place. There were also awards made under the Grand Duchy of Warsaw 1807-1813, a French sponsored "state".

After the downfall of Napoleon I, the Kingdom of Poland was set up (1815-1831), under Emperor Alexander I as ruler. During this time period Polish awards were still given but mainly to Russians, according to Wesolowski, see below. In 1831, after a failed rebellion, all pretense at a separate Poland was dropped. The Orders of the White Eagle and St Stanislaus became Imperial Russian Orders, while the Virtuti Militari became obsolete.

In 1918 after the communists had taken over Russia, Poland became independent again and reintroduced the White Eagle and Virtuti Militari, but not St Stanislaus. The Order of Polonia Restituta (Restored Poland) was created.

129

For further reading on this subject it is recommended that you consult **POLISH ORDERS, MEDALS, BADGES AND INSIGNIA, MILITARY AND CIVILIAN DECORATIONS 1705-1985** by Zdzislaw P. Wesolowski.

Early issues of the post 1918 Virtuti Militari were numbered on the reverse. During World War II, Polish awards were made in France, Italy, Palestine, and Great Britain.

The British firm of Spink & Son Ltd made awards for the Polish Government in Exile, during World War II. After the war a government in exile was reconstituted when the communists took over in Poland. The status of these items is questionable. Now that there is a non-communist government again the position of the items perhaps is different.

During the communist period the Order of Polonia Restituta was continued but with the date 1944 replacing 1918, and the eagle on the obverse being uncrowned.

The Orders of the White Eagle, and Virtuti Militari of the 1918 type have been copied. However, some of these were made in Britain during World War II and should be regarded as genuine. For the most part Polish awards have not been hallmarked. Stars of Polonia Restituta, British made, may have a back plate referring to manufacture by Spink & Son Ltd, by appointment to HM King George VI, and Queen Elizabeth II.

With the overthrow of the communist regime Polish awards have resumed their previous appearance.

The Orders of Poland include: White Eagle, Virtuti Militari, Saint Stanislaus, and Polonia Restituta (Restored Poland).

PORTUGAL
Monarchy from the middle ages; republic in 1911.

The Orders, Medals and Decorations of this country like many others have differences in appearance according to their period of issue. Thus, early Portuguese Orders of the 18th and 19th centuries look considerably different to the 20th century issues. Compounding this is the reissue in somewhat altered form of the awards of the Republic after 1911. Many new Orders were also established which gives Portugal, for a small country, an extensive system of awards.

Except for the World War I War Cross, and the Victory Medal, there does not seem to be a problem of copies.

Some of the jewelers are Joao Anjus, da Costa, and Souza. The finer republican pieces appear to have been made by da Costa. The firm of Souza makes many of the current Portuguese insignia.

The Orders of Portugal include: Combined Honor Award of the Three Orders, Christ (see also Vatican State), Benedict of Aviz, James of the Sword, Tower and Sword, Villa Vicosa, St Isabella, Henry the Navigator,

130

Imperial Order, Civil Merit, Military Merit, Public Instruction, Agricultural Merit (green enamel), Industrial Merit (red enamel). The last two are identical in design, but with different color enamel as noted.

RUMANIA
Monarchy after independence from Turkey in 1878; People's Republic in 1947.

The Orders, Medals and Decorations of this country reflect several influences. Some of the Orders come in a multitude of classes, with and without swords which has its origins in Germany. The use of rosettes on the IV Class of Orders, and their designation as the grade of Officer; the II Classes being referred to as Grand Officer are French in origin.

The Rumanian House Order of Hohenzollern is an offshoot of the Princely and Royal Prussian Hohenzollern House Orders.

There are copies of the Order of Carol I and the World War I Victory Medal. The two major jewelers were Monetaria Nationala (National Mint), and Resch of Bucharest.

The Orders of this country include: King Carol, Michael the Brave, Ferdinand I, St George, Merit, Faithful Service, the Star (two types), the Crown (two types), Royal Household (Hohenzollern), Bene-Merenti, Agricultural Merit, Cultural Merit, Air Force Bravery, and the Honor decoration of the Rumanian Eagle.

Type I of the Crown Order can be identified by the crown being on the obverse centre of the badges, with the initial "C" reversed and correct between the arms. For type II the crown appears between the arms of the cross and the cipher is on the obverse centre.

RUSSIA
Empire till 1917, followed by a Provisional Republican Government 1917, and a communist government from 1917 to 1989, and then a democratic republic.

Prior to December 1916, all badges of Imperial Russian Orders were gold and enamel. The gold content was usually marked by the number 56, (56 parts out of 96, and thus roughly equivalent to 14 carat gold.) Breast Stars were silver and enamel, and marked with a silver content number usually 84 (84 parts out of 96, which corresponds to 875 fineness, or below the common European sterling of 925 parts out of 1000.)

Most of the Imperial Orders on the market date from the late 19th and early 20th centuries. The two major jewelers were Eduard, and Keibel. The badges of the Orders are very similar, but the breast stars are distinctively different. The Eduard stars are vaulted, or much higher in the centre when laid down than the Keibel stars which are quite flat.

When awarding an Order to a non-Christian the Russian practice was to replace the centre with the Imperial eagle. This has led to the recent appearance of many pieces of questionable status. Since the non-Christian pieces are rarer, and thus more valuable, it has been worthwhile for some enterprising forger to make replacement centres of the Imperial eagle and apply them to the common variety of insignia.

Badges of the Imperial Russian Orders (and the Provisional Government) after December 1916 were bronze/gilt and enamels, but never silver/gilt. A silver/gilt Imperial Russian Order is either a piece made in France after the Russian Revolution, during the emigration, or a copy, or a fake, depending on which word you would rather use.

Badges of Soviet Russian Orders were die struck with the legend equivalent to the House of the Mint (Moscow), or Leningrad House of the Mint, with a serial number engraved below. Small red covered books were issued, listing the specific serial number, and the recipient.

Soviet awards were not marked as to precious metal content. Thus, if one find a piece like the Order of the Patriotic War marked 800 (for silver content) then you know it's a fake.

The Orders of Imperial Russia included: St Andrew, St Catherine, St Alexander Nevsky, White Eagle, St George St Vladimir, St Anne, St Stanislas, Agricultural Merit, and St John (Knights of Malta). The last two are rare.

The Orders of Soviet Russia included: Lenin, October Revolution, Victory, Red Banner, Suvorov, Ushakov, Kutuzov, Nakhimov, Bohdan Khmelnitsky, Alexander Nevsky, Patriotic War, Red Star, Glory, Honor (Badge of Honor), Red Banner of Labor, and Motherhood Glory.

It should be noted that Soviet Orders exist in several different styles. Some originated hanging from small rectangular red ribbons, were altered to a screw back form, and then were converted to a standard Soviet ribbon suspension. The Soviet Order of Glory uses the same orange and black striped ribbon as the Imperial Order of St George.

SAN MARINO
A republic since early modern times.

This tiny country nestled in northern Italy has the Orders of St Agatha and San Marino. They are identified later in this work. Presumably they have been made in Italy at various times. Copies of these items do not appear to be a problem.

SLOVAKIA
A Nazi puppet state from 1938-1944; reestablished as a republic after the break up of Czechoslovakia in the 1990's.

After the bloodless occupation of the Sudetenland in March 1938, the movement for Slovakian secession from the republic of Czechoslovakia led to the establishment of a puppet state of Slovakia, under III Reich supervision.

This "state" issued its own Orders, Medals, and Decorations, which are referred to in the identification section. Most of its awards appeared to have been made in Germany, and it is known that there are copies of the Prince Pribina Order. All Slovak material is scarce or rare, but the shadow of copies exists.

The Orders of Slovakia include: the Order of Prince Pribina, the Order of the Slovak Cross, and the Order of the War Victory Cross.

SPAIN

A monarchy until 1931; republic till 1939; dictatorship from 1939-1976 when the monarchy was restored.

The Order, Medals, and Decorations of this country have gone through many upheavals as has the history of the country. Civil wars, revolutions and other events have contributed to the variation in Spanish awards.

The Spanish monarchy persisted until 1931 when a republic was proclaimed. Civil War broke out in 1936 when General Francisco Franco invaded Spain from Morocco. After three years, with German and Italian aid he was able to overthrow the republic. Franco ruled until his death in 1976, when the monarchy was restored again.

In modern times (20th century) Spanish Orders can be distinguished in at least two distinct types. Of course this applies to those Orders in use during the monarchy and the Franco dictatorship. The royal pieces were suspended from a royal crown, (where appropriate), with arches and a top with a cross, while the Franco pieces from a coronet, which is essentially a rather low band of metal with a cutout top edge, and no arches.

Some Spanish Orders have the fleur-de-ly on them which might make some think that they are French. However, this is just a symbol of the Bourbon royal family, shared with France. Spain also has the unique distinction of using small breast stars for the lower classes of its Orders. This can be confusing for the collector because for all other countries a breast star indicates the I or II class. Most Spanish Orders are numbered in reverse, so the I Class would be lowest, a breast cross, and the highest would be the IV Class, equivalent to the Grand Cross of other Orders with a badge on a sash, with a breast star.

Spanish Orders have been issued in so many variations that it may be difficult to tell their time period. Quality of enamel is a clue, as is size. Older insignia tend to be small.

Spain also issued many medals for a variety of activities. Of interest to the British collector are those created for the Napoleonic campaigns, corresponding to the bars for the Military General Service Medal. Of interest to the American collector are the medals for Cuba and the Philippines. Intriguing is that Winston Churchill was awarded the Military Merit Order for being an observer in Cuba in 1895 during one of the periodic uprisings against Spanish rule.

The Military Merit, Naval Merit, and Air Forces Merit Orders need some particular attention since they can come in four variations.

1. In red enamel for combat/wartime service.

2. The same-but with colored bars on the arms of insignia to indicate an award with a pension.

3. In white enamel for non-combat/peacetime service.

4. The same-but with colored bars on the arms of the insignia to indicate an award with a pension.

A wide range of jewelers have made Spanish Orders. Halley of Paris is well known for some exquisite breast stars. Two of the principal jewelers have been Juan Medina, maker of the Royal Orders during the mid-19th into the early 20th century, and Mariano Cejalvo.

The Orders of Spain include: Golden Fleece (see also Austria), Charles III, Isabella the Catholic, St Ferdinand, St Hermengildo, Military Merit, Naval Merit, Air Force Merit, Maria Christina, Alfonso XII, Civil Merit, Charity, Agricultural Merit, Red Cross Merit, Republic Merit, Yoke and Arrows, Alfonso X, Cisneros, St Raymond of Penafort, Africa, Health and the War Cross. In addition there are breast stars for some officials under the pre-1931 monarchy, notably for Judges.

SWEDEN
Monarchy since the middle ages.

The awards of this country continue to be made to a high standard. The badges of Orders are most often found in gold, and apparently were made so for much longer than most other countries.

The breast "stars" of the Orders are actually large silver crosses which look somewhat alike. The Order of the Sword is surely one of the most beautiful created.

The major jeweler of this country is C.F.Carlman of Stockman, with his insignia being marked CFC. There does not seem to be a problem with copies.

The Orders of Sweden include: Seraphim, North Star, Vasa, and the Sword.

UNITED STATES OF AMERICA
Republic since 1776.

This country once was the stingiest in granting awards to its armed forces, and civilian officials. It has gone to the opposite extreme with a vast array of items for both sectors. Each department , and many of the agencies of the federal government have a variety of medals. The armed forces also have a panoply of decorations for gallantry, some of which they share. However, there is sometimes confusion for the collector when one examines some of the citations on which awards are based. Gallantry is a subjective matter. Each service has its own standards and judgements as to its nature.

To make it clear to the reader, below are listed the gallantry and merit awards of the United States Armed Forces.

GALLANTRY AWARDS-Combat
Note: Repeat awards by the Army and Air Force are indicated by the addition of an oak leaf cluster to the ribbon of the award. The Navy, Marine Corps and the Coast Guard use a gold star for the same purpose. The Coast Guard awards U.S. Navy gallantry decorations under combat or wartime conditions.

Medal of Honor (not the often used "Congressional" Medal of Honor):
Army-began as a breast decoration during the Civil War; continued as such in a new form in 1904; become a neck decoration in 1940's; ribbon has varied.
Navy-basic design unchanged from inception; the ribbon has varied.
Air Force-2 types; one with the maker's initials on the reverse at 6 o'clock HLP (His Lordship Products-[later to be LI-Lordship Industries-but not to be inscribed on the decoration]; the other -with a blank reverse.

Distinguished Service Cross-several types-on split wrap, wrap, slot, and crimped brooches, the latter after World War II.
Navy Distinguished Service Medal-When first established during World War I this award was senior to the Navy Cross for gallantry. Later it came to have the same status as the Army medal.
Navy Cross-several types-one very distinctive with blackened appearance (known as the "Black Widow")-see remarks above.
Air Force Cross-2 types-first with initials HLP on edge of left arm (see USAF Medal of Honor above.)

Silver Star-thick and thin types; numbered and unnumbered.

Combat/non-combat gallantry decorations
Distinguished Flying Cross-navy type-frosted appearance-wrap brooch;
shiny Army (Air Corps) type-slot brooch, which later superseded the navy
issue, but on a crimped brooch.
Legion of Merit-with V for valor-several types.
Bronze Star-with a V.
Commendation Medals-with a V.

Non-combat gallantry awards
Distinguished Flying Cross
Soldiers' Medal-numbered and unnumbered; some are found named.
Navy and Marine Corps Medal.
Airmen's Medal.
Coast Guard Medal.

Defense Department Awards
Distinguished Service Medal
Superior Service Medal
Meritorious Service Medal

Distinguished Service Medals
Army-basic design unchanged; early issues numbered; sometimes found
named.
Navy-type I-although struck, and awarded to some foreign admirals during
World War I, was abandoned in favor of type two, the style still awarded.
Navy Cross-when first instituted in World War I was primarily an award for
distinguished service, and inferior to the Navy D.S.M. Later it became the
second highest naval gallantry decoration.
Air Force
Coast Guard

Awards for Meritorious Service
Legion of Merit-primarily an officers' award.
Bronze Star
Air Medal
Meritorious Service Medal

Commendation Medals
Army-originally known as the Commendation ribbon, then so with metal
pendant.
Navy
Air Force
Coast Guard-three types
Joint Service

Achievement Medals
Army
Navy
Air Force
Coast Guard
Joint Service

All awards to the Navy are also granted to the Marine Corps. Those awards designated as Joint Service are granted by the Defense Department, as opposed to the individual service departments.

Campaign and Service Medals fall into several categories. The issues prior to World War II were, with few exceptions, numbered on the rim with one of three systems: 1. A number with prefix "No."; 2.A number with prefix "M No."; 3. A number without prefix. The first two were struck by the U.S. Mint, the others by private companies. Campaign and Service Medals from World War II on were issued unnumbered.

Two medals from the Spanish American War, the Manila Bay (Dewey) Medal, and the West Indies Naval Campaign (Sampson) Medal were officially named, and are easy to verify as medal rolls of recipients exist.

Many Campaign and Service Medals were reissued unnumbered, and some were reissued with an extruded loop (knob) suspension instead of the original ring.

The general rule was that when all branches, Army, Navy and Marine Corps were present there were different medals that reflected that, rather than one design for all. The Navy and Marine Corps medals had identical obverses, but distinctive reverses.

Additionally, to commemorate a host of smaller campaign actions, the U. S. Navy, and the U.S.M.C. both established an expeditionary medal. These medals, unnumbered for the Navy, and originally numbered for the Marine Corps, can be found with the bar WAKE ISLAND commemorating the epic defense of that island against the Japanese in World War II.

The Army and Air Force Good Conduct Medals are identical except for their ribbons. Prior to the emergence of the separate USAF, air force personnel received the army medal. The Navy, Marine Corps and the Coast Guard originally employed a system of bars worn on the medal ribbon to denote additional periods of service beyond the original issue of the medal. These medals originally were named with some details of service or station.

At one time, these and some marksmanship awards were the only medals being worn by U.S. servicemen.

The production of U.S. awards has been an odd combination of public and private. Some items have been produced by the U.S. Mint. Some by private companies using dies or hubs provided by the U.S. Mint, while some have been wholly produced by private firms. Among the firms which have produced U.S. awards are Bailey, Banks and Biddle; Bastian Bros.; Whitehead and Hoag; GRACO; Medallic Art Co.; HLP (His Lordship Products); LI (Lordship Industries) to name some.

The United States has no Orders in the European sense. However, the multi-class Legion of Merit performs the same function.

Since World War II design of U.S. awards largely has been in the hands of the Institute of Heraldry. In this author's opinion this has not contributed to the improvement of medallic art.

VATICAN STATE (also Papal States)

In the religious sense the Vatican State is the religious heir of the Western Roman Empire. The territories of the Roman Catholic Church were incorporated in a united Italy in 1870. In 1929 Mussolini, the Italian Dictator, negotiated a political status for Church properties in Rome which have come to have official recognition from most of the other nations of the world.

The Orders of the Vatican State, successor to the Papal States are very colorful in appearance. One Order, the Order of Christ is shared with Portugal. There is also a variation of the insignia of the Knights of Malta. Vatican insignia have been made by jewelers from several countries. Medals for the most part bear the effigy of a reigning pope, and are thus easy to identify .

The Orders of the Vatican (and Papal States) include: Holy Sepulchre, St Sylvester and the Golden Spur, St Sylvester; Christ (see Portugal), St Gregory, and Pius. The military version of the Order of the Holy Sepulchre appears with a "trophy of arms" suspension. The Order of St Gregory appears in both military and civil types. The former suspended by a "trophy of arms" and the latter from an enameled wreath.

REPUBLIC OF VIETNAM (South)

French colony until 1954 when split into two countires; the north a Communist state and the south a pro-Western one.

In the earliest period some awards were made in France. As an example, the Army Gallantry Cross can be found with the reverse of the suspension marked "France". Early issues of the Military Merit Medal bear the head of the former Emperor of Annam (Vietnam) Bao Dai.

Most awards, however, are of Vietnamese or U.S. manufacture. Neither are of exceptionally high quality but the Vietnamese ones generally have a poorer appearance and the ribbons are of a coarse material. Most U.S. made versions were produced under contract with the U.S. armed forces and thus do not fall into the usual category of copies.

138

WORLD WAR I VICTORY MEDALS

Awarded after the 1914-18 War. Originally known as the Great War for Civilization, and now referred to as World War I.

This is one of the most collectible and popular series of medals. For a detailed analysis of this series the reader is directed to Alexander J. Laslo's **THE INTERALLIED VICTORY MEDALS OF WORLD WAR I**. This work has done so much for the collector in terms of straightening out myths and fiction regarding these medals. The countries awarding them were: Belgium, Brazil, Cuba, Czechoslovakia, France, Great Britain, Greece, Italy, Japan, Portugal, Rumania, Siam, Union of South Africa, United States of America.

The British and S. African were both officially named to the recipient. The two medals are identical on the obverse; with the British having the reverse legend in English only, with the S. African in English & Afrikaans. The United States used its medal as a war commemorative, and also as a campaign medal with a variety of bars slipped over the ribbon. These bars have been extensively copied.

Many of the different medals have been copied. In addition there are unofficial varieties, and rejected designs. According to an article in the July 1995 MEDAL COLLECTOR by Nat Futterman, there have been identified at least 100 varieties, official and otherwise of this series.

YUGOSLAVIA

Includes Serbia, Montenegro, Croatia, Kingdom of Yugoslavia.

The Orders, Medals and decorations of Croatia, from the World War II period can be identified fairly easily as their inscriptions are in the Roman alphabet, see elsewhere. The awards of Montenegro and Serbia are more difficult because of their inscriptions being in Cyrillic. Before World War I Serbian and Montenegrin awards tended to be made in Austria by Scheid, among others, while after the war, Hueguenin of Switzerland became the jeweler for the Orders of St Sava of Serbia/Yugoslavia, and of the Crown of Yugoslavia. Montenegro had been absorbed into Yugoslavia and its awards ceased to exist.

The Order of St Sava exists in three types. 1.Saint with red robes; reverse cipher. 2.Saint with red robes; reverse date 1883. 3.Saint's robes yellow/green; reverse date 1883.

Both Montenegro and Serbia had a Milosh Oblitch Medal for Bravery. Only the name was the same. The medals were very different, while the Serbian medal was the more common.

The Orders of Yugoslavia include: St Sava (carried over from Serbia); and the Crown.

CHAPTER VI

INTERNATIONAL JEWELERS

In the previous chapter dealing with individual countries reference has been made to jewelers. In addition it is important to note that there were some jewelers who made Orders for a number of countries, other than their own. One should realize that just because one can identify a maker's name or initials that does not mean that one has identified the country awarding it, although sometimes it is a clue. The list below is not be complete, but it will give an idea of what may be found. For further reference see **COURT JEWELERS OF THE WORLD** by Jeffrey Jacob.

Arthus Bertrand-Paris, France
Many countries such as Serbia, Montenegro, Greece.

Karl Fischmeister-Vienna, Austria
Serbian Orders including Takovo and St Sava.

Garrard-London, Great Britain
Many Commonwealth countries, and associated such as Orders of Sudan, Iraq (royal), and Jordan.

Godet-Berlin, Germany
Orders of all the German States, as well as many foreign countries, such as Russia, China, Portugal, Spain. Very high quality work.

Halley-Paris, France
Spain-Isabella the Catholic, Charles III; Persian Lion and Sun; Turkish Orders.

Huguenin Freres et Cie, Le Locle-Switzerland
Finland, Greece, Serbia, Yugoslavia-post World War I, to name some.

Kretly-Paris, France
Orders from Portugal, Turkey, Brazil, Vatican .

Lemaitre-Paris, France
Most European Orders.

Vinc Meyer-Vienna, Austria
Papal Orders and decorations; Serbian Takovo; Greek Redeemer among many.

C.F.Rothe & Neffe-Vienna, Austria
Made original insignia of many countries' awards, including many of the
German states pre-1918; also made some excellent copies. Some fine
examples of the latter are Russian Order of St George, and the Prussian
Pour Le Mérite.

G.A.Schied-Vienna, Austria
Serbian White Eagle, Takovo, and St Sava

Johan Schwerdtner-Vienna, Austria
Bulgarian Civil and Military Merit Orders.

Rudolf Souval-Vienna, Austria
Orders of Greece, and Rumania; badges for the III Reich marked RS.

Spink & Son-London, Great Britain
Awards for many governments in exile during World War II; many
Commonwealth and other foreign countries.

CHAPTER VII

IDENTIFYING ORDERS, MEDALS AND DECORATIONS

One of the most frustrating things that can happen to a collector is that at some time he/she will come across something mysterious. "What is it?" "Where can I find out about it?" It doesn't matter what country or aspect of a country one collects; it will happen. You buy a collection from someone; you buy a lot in an auction; you go to a flea market or antique show; and there it is!

There is a tendency to ignore items that you don't collect. However, there is also the tendency to engage in amateur commercial activity, buying and selling on the side to augment one's own ability to collect. The answer to this dilemma is relatively simple. All you need is a reference which will answer all your questions, with lots of pictures and explanations. Unfortunately, this reference does not exist. Thus, one needs to have a variety of references, which may have overlapping material, and access to "experts" who may be of assistance. Collectors' organizations may help also.

Perhaps the best way to learn is to ask many questions about what you see. The question you don't ask is one that is not going to be answered. Pick up and handle as much material as possible. Always have a powerful magnifying glass, and a notebook with you to record observations. The glass, because many details are not readily discernible to the naked eye, and the notebook because you may not remember what you saw! There always are clues that can assist in identifying an item; an inscription or legend; a bar or clasp on the ribbon; a symbol on the obverse or reverse; the profile of a monarch or some other person.

The ribbon is often a clue as to identity, but one must be careful. There have been many awards that have appeared with the wrong ribbon. Obviously, relying on the ribbon alone can be very misleading.

The material below is an attempt to provide some useful clues to identifying Orders, Medals and Decorations from around the world. However, due to limitations beyond the author's control this applies generally to the awards of countries using the alphabets of the western world. Symbols used by various countries, as well as some identifying legends will be listed. Some symbols were used by several countries.

SYMBOLS APPEARING ON AWARDS
Note: Symbols may appear in a variety of places; as part of the suspension, between the arms of a cross, on the obverse, on the reverse.

Crown

Note: Because there are so many Orders that bear a crown in some way, usually as part of their suspension, it was decided to list only those Orders specifically known as the Order of the Crown.

Austria
Order of the Iron Crown.

Belgium
Order of the Crown.

France
Order of the Iron Crown.

Germany
Bavaria-Order of the Bavarian Crown.
Mecklenburg-Order of the Wendish Crown.
Prussia-Merit Order of the Prussian Crown; Order of the Crown.
Saxony-Order of the Rue Crown.
Westphalia-Order of the Crown of Westphalia.
Wuerttemberg-Order of the Crown of Wuerttemberg.

Hawaii
Royal Order of the Crown of Hawaii.

Hungary
Order of the Holy Crown of St Stephen.

Italy
Order of the Crown

Japan
Order of the Sacred Crown.

Rumania
Order of the Crown.

Double Headed Eagle

Albania
Order of Scanderbeg, Order of Fidelity.

Austria
Empire-Order of the Iron Crown, Order of Franz Joseph, Order of the Starry
Cross.
I Republic-some insignia of the Merit Order-uncrowned eagles.

Montenegro
Order of St Peter; Medal for Bravery.

Russia
Empire-Order of St Andrew, Order of St Alexander Nevsky, Order of the
White Eagle (also see Poland), Order of St Stanislas, Cross of St George
(non-Christian recipients), Crosses and Medals for Polish Rebellion 1831,
Pacification of Hungary 1849, Service Cross for Caucasus 1864, Polish
Rebellion 1864.
Provisional Government-Order of St Stanislas-eagles uncrowned.

Serbia
Order of the White Eagle, Order of St Sava,; Order of Karageorge, Medal
for Zeal.

Dragon

Annam (French Colonial)
Order of the Dragon.

China
Order of the Double Dragon.

Japan-Manchukuo
Order of the Illustrious Dragon.

Elephant

Denmark
Order of the Elephant.

Laos
Order of the Million Elephants and White Parasol.

Thailand
Order of the Elephant.

Falcon

Germany
Saxe-Weimar-Order of the White Falcon.

Iceland
Order of the Falcon

George Washington

U.S.A.-Purple Heart.

Griffin

Finland
Order of the White Rose.

Germany
Mecklenburg-Order of the Griffin.

Russia
Order of Agricultural Merit.

Hammer and Sickle

Most of the awards of the Soviet Union.
Most of the awards of East European Communist countries, except for East
Germany.

Horse

Germany
Brunswick-Order of Henry the Lion.

Great Britain
Order of St John

Lion

Belgium
Order of Leopold, Order of Leopold II, Order of the Lion of the Congo,
various other medals.

Bulgaria
Order of Saint Alexander, Royal Military Order, various other crosses and medals.

Czechoslovakia
Order of the White Lion, Military Order of the White Lion.

Ethiopia
Order of Menelik II.

Finland
Order of the Lion, Medals of Liberty-silver and bronze.

Germany
Baden-Order of the Zahringen Lion
Bavaria-Military Merit Order
Hannover-Guelphic Order
Hesse (Electoral)-Order of the Golden Lion, Order of William.
Saxon Duchies-Saxe-Ernestine House Order.

Great Britain
Victoria Cross, Order of the Bath-military, Guelphic Order, Order of British India.

Luxemburg
Order of Adolph, Order of the Resistance.

Netherlands
Order of the Union of Holland, Order of Orange Nassau, (there is an Order of the Netherlands Lion, but there is no lion on the insignia.)

Norway
Order of Saint Olav.

Persia (Iran)
Order of the Lion and Sun.

Phoenix

Germany
Hohenlohe-Order of the Phoenix.

Greece
Order of the Phoenix.

Rose

Brazil
Order of the Rose

Finland
Order of the White Rose, Liberty Cross Order.

Germany
Lippe & Schaumburg-Lippe-Honor Cross of the Lippe House.

Saint George and the Dragon

Germany
Bavaria-Order of St George.
Hannover-Order of St George.

Great Britain
Order of the Garter, Order of St Michael and St George, George Cross,
George Medal.

Italy
Parma-Order of Constantine.
Two Sicilies (Naples)-Order of St George of the Reunion.

Russia
Empire-Order of St George, Cross of St George.
Provisional Government-Medal of St George.

Single Headed Eagle

Austria
II Republic-Order of the Decoration of Honor (Order of Merit).

Estonia
Order of the Cross of the Eagle.

France
Order of the Three Golden Fleece, Order of the Iron Crown (see also
Austrian Empire), Legion of Honor-Napoleon I & Napoleon III, Medaille
Militaire-Napoleon III-types I & II.

Germany

III Reich-Order of the German Eagle; also present in various forms on many badges and awards.

Federal Republic-Merit Order.

Prussia-Pour Le Mérite, Order of the Black Eagle, Order of the Red Eagle Johanniter Order, Hohenzollern House Order, Hohenzollern Campaign 1849.

Westphalia-Order of the Crown.

Italy

States

Modena-Order of the Eagle of Este.

Two Sicilies (Naples)-Order of the Two Sicilies.

Monarchy

Order of the Roman Eagle.

Republic

Order of Merit.

Mexico

Monarchy-Order of the Mexican Eagle, Order of Guadalupe.

Republic-Order of the Aztec Eagle.

Philippines

Medal for Valor, Distinguished Conduct Star.

Poland

Kingdom-Order of the White Eagle, Order of St Stanislaus.

Republic-Order of the White Eagle, Order of Polonia Restituta.

Rumania

Order of Carol I, Order of the Star, Hohenzollern House Order, Aeronautical Merit Order, Order for the Militia, and various other medals.

Spain

Order of Cisneros, Colonial Order of Africa.

United States of America

Medal of Honor-Army, Distinguished Service Cross, Distinguished Service Medal-Army and Navy; Certificate of Merit Medal, National Defense Service Medal, many civilian awards bear the traditional American eagle.

148

Star

France-Colonial
Benin-Order of the Black Star.

Latvia
Order of the Three Stars.

Sweden
Order of the North Star.

U.S.A.
Legion of Merit, Presidential Medal of Freedom.

Swastika

Finland
Order of the White Rose-Collar-type I, Liberty Cross Order.

Germany-III Reich
Appears on most of the awards.

Latvia
Order of the Bearslayer.

LEGENDS AND INSCRIPTIONS APPEARING ON AWARDS

Introductory Note: Not every medal issued and dated is listed below. Where the information on the medal clearly identifies the item there is no point in belaboring the issue. However, the material below does take into account that we all have different linguistic strengths.

For the most part, the inscription is found on the reverse.

1. The Roman Alphabet - this covers the countries in Europe using it, as well as the the United States of America.

AFRICA ORIENTALE MOLTI NEMICI MOLTO HONORE-Italy-Ethiopian Campaign Medal 1945.
AFRICA SERVICE MEDAL-AFRIKA DIENS-MEDALJE-Union of South Africa-Africa Service Medal World War II.
A HAZAERT-Hungary-National Defense Cross 1940; Fire Cross (Frontline Service Cross 1941.)
A HONVEDELEMERT 1944-Hungary-Civil Defense Service Cross 1944.

A LA LEALTAD ACRISOLADA-For unqualified loyalty-Spain-Order of Isabella the Catholic.

ALFONSO X EL SABIO, REY DE CASTILLA Y DE LEON-Alfonso X the Wise, King of Castile and Leon-Spain-Order of Alfonso X.

AL MERITO CIVIL-For civil merit-Spain-Civil Merit Order.

AL MERITO DI LUNGO COMANDO-Italy-Army Long Service Medal.

AL MERITO COLONIALE-Colonial Merit-Italy-Colonial Merit Order.

AL MERITO EN CAMPANA-For merit in the field-Spain-Order of Maria Cristina.

AL MERITO LAVORO-Labor Merit-Italy-Order of Labor Merit.

AL MERITO MILITARE-For Military Merit-Spain-Order of St Ferdinand

AL MERITO SANITARIO-For Public Health Merit-Spain-Order of Public Health.

ALTIORA PETO-I seek higher things-Spain-Order of Alfonso XII.

AL VALORE CIVILE-Civil Valor-Italy-Civil Order of Savoy; Medal of Civil Valor.

AL VALORE MILITARE-Military Valor-Italy-Military Order of Savoy; Military Valor Medal.

ALBERTUS ANIMOSUS-Albert the Bold-Germany-Saxony-Order of Albert.

ALTIOR ADVERSIS-Against all odds-German-Mecklenburg-Order of the Griffin (breast star).

AL MERITO Y VIRTUDES-For merit and virtue-Mexico-Order of Guadalupe-reverse of civil badge.

AL PATRIOTISMO HEROICO-For patriotic heroism-Mexico-Order of Guadalupe-reverse of military badge.

A MAGYAR FELVIDEK...-Hungary-Upper Hungary Commemorative Medal 1938.

AMAN. JUST. PIET. FID.-To those who love justice, piety and fidelity-Russia-Order of St Anne-breast star.

AMOR E FEDELIDADE-Love and fidelity-Brazil-Order of the Rose.

ANDENKEN AN DIE HULDIGUNG 12.AUG.1838-Austria-Tirol Gratitude Medal-1838.

AN BONN SEIRBHIS-Ireland-The Service Medal 1944.

AN FORSA COSANTA AITUIL-The Local Defence Force-Ireland-Emergency Service Medal 1939-1946.

AN SERBHIS SEIPLINEACHTA - The Chaplaincy Service - Ireland-Emergency Service Medal 1939-1946.

AN SLUA MUIRI-For the naval reserve-Ireland-Emergency Service Medal 1939-1946.

AN TSEIRBHIS MHUIR-TRACTALA-The Merchant Marine Service-Ireland-Merchant Marine Service Medal 1939-1946.

ARMEE MÉRITE ANCIENNES-Army Long Service-Belgium-Army Long Service Cross.

ARMY OF OCCUPATION- with castle on obverse- U.S.A.- Army of Occupation Medal for World War II.

ARTES LETRAS INDUSTRIA CIENCIAS-Arts,letters, industry and science-Spain-Order of Maria Vittoria.

ASCENDIMUS VIGILANDO-Ascending by vigilance-Germany-Saxe-Weimar-Order of the White Falcon.

ATAVIS ET ARMIS-By ancestors and arms-France-Order of St Lazarus and Our Lady of Mount Carmel.

AUSPICIUM MELIORIS AEVI-An omen of a better time-Great Britain-Order of St Michael and St George.

AUX DEFENSEURS DE LA PATRIE-To the Defenders of the Fatherland-France 1870-1871-Franco-Prussian War Medal (reverse-large & small size).

AVITA ET AUCTA-Heritage and Progress-Austria-Order of the Iron Crown.

AVITO VIRET HONORE-We thrive in ancestral honor-Germany-Mecklenburg-Strelitz-Order of the Wendish Crown.

B on red triangle-Belgium-Cross for Political Prisoners 1940-45.

BARBATIE SI CREDINTA-Rumania-Medal for Manliness and Loyalty.

BELL(ICAE) VIRTUTIS PRAEMIUM-Award for warlike virtue-France-Order of St Louis.

BENEMERENCIA-Merit-Portugal-Order of Merit.

BENE MERENTI-Award for Merit-Rumania-Merit Medal; House Order.

BENE MERENTI-Award for Merit-Vatican & Papal States-Merit Medal.

BENE MERENTIUM PRAEMIUM-Awarded for Merit-Brazil-Order of the Southern Cross-type I.

BOG I HRVATI-God and the Croatians-Croatia-Order of the Crown of Zvonimir.

CAESARIS CAESARI DEI DEO-Render unto Caesar the things that are Caesar's, and to God the things that are God's-Spain-Order of the Yoke and Arrows.

CAMPAGNA ITALO-TEDESCA IN AFRICA - ITALIENSCH-DEUTSCHER FELDZUG IN AFRIKA-Italian-German Campaign Medal for N. Africa-Italy-unofficial medal for the N. African Campaign World War II-given to German forces in the Afrika Corps.

CAMPANHAS DO EXERCITO PORTUGUES 1916-Portugese Army campaign-Portugese Campaign Medal 1916-18.

CANADA-Great Britain-Canada General Service Medal 1866-70.

CAOMNOIRI AITIULA-Local Security Forces-Ireland-Emergency Service Medal 1939-46.

CAROLA KOENIGIN VON SACHSEN-Germany-Saxony-Queen Carola Medal World War I.

CESKOSLOVENSKA ARMADA V ZAHRANICI 1939/1945-The Czechoslovak Army abroad-Czechoslovakia-World War II Commemorative Medal.

CHARAKTER UND AUFRICHTIGKEIT-Character and straightforwardness-Germany-Westphalia-Order of the Crown.

CHINA-Great Britain-China 1857-1860.

CONFORTAMINI ET PUGNATE-Gather your strength and fight-Latvia-Order of Vesthardus-reverse of badge.

CROCE AL VALOR MILITARE-Italy-Cross for Military Valor.

CROCE DI GUERRA-War Cross-Italy-War Cross.

CROIX DE GUERRE LEGIONNAIRE-Vichy France-reverse of the French Volunteer Legion War Cross 1941.

CRUX RUBRA HUNGARICA 1922-Hungary-reverse of Red Cross awards.

CSR-with two soldiers-Czechoslovakia-Merit Medal.

DANSK KRIGSFANGERHJAELP 1914-1919-Denmark-Red Cross Medal for Prisoner of War Aid.

DANSK RODE KORS 1939-45-Denmark-Danish Red Cross Commemorative Medal 1939-45.

DAS LAND TIROL DEN VERTEIDIGERN DES VATERLANDES 1914-18-Austria-Defense of the Tirol 1914-18.

DE GEEST OVERWINT-Netherlands- East Asia Resistance Star World War II.

DE GROOTE OOLOG TOT BESCHAVING - LA GRANDE GUERRE POUR LA CIVILIZATION-The Great War for Civilization (in Flemish and French)-Belgium-World War I Victory Medal.

DEM MILITAIR-VERDIENSTE-Germany-Lippe-Military Merit Medal World War I.

DEM TAPFEREN-Germany-Baden-Karl-Friedrich Military Merit Medal.

DEM TIROLER LANDESVERTHEIDIGER 1848-Defense of the Tirol 1848-Austria-Tirol Commemorative Medal 1848.

DEM VERDIENSTE-For Merit-Germany/Waldeck-Civil Merit Order.

DEM VERDIENSTE 1914-Germany/Saxe-Weimar- Eisenach-General Decoration of Honor.

DEN TAPFEREN VERTEIDIGERN DES VATERLANDES MCCCXCVII-For the brave defense of the Fatherland-1797-Austria-Defense of the fatherland 1797.

DEN VADERLANT GHETROUWE-Netherlands-reverse of the Mobilization Cross World War II.

DE REGE OPTIME MERITO-High merit from the king-Italy-Sicily-Royal Order of Francis I.

DER TAPFERKEIT-For Bravery-Austria-Bravery Medals.

DE TYRANNY VERDRYVEN-Netherlands-Resistance Memorial Cross.

DEUTSCHE VERDIENST-MEDAILLE-Germany/III Reich-Merit Medal of the German Eagle Order.

DIE V. OCT. MCMVII IN MEMORIAM-In commemoration of the 5th October 1908-Austria-Medal for the annexation of Bosnia-Herzegovina.

DIN CARPATI PESTE DUNARE LA BALCANI-From the Carpathians over the Danube into the Balkans-Rumania-Second Balkan War Medal 1913 (reverse).

DISTINGUISHED SERVICE-U.S.A.-Navy and Coast Guard Distinguished Service Medals.

DIVISION ESPANOLA DE VOLUNTARIOS IN RUSIA-Spanish division of volunteers in Russia-Germany-III Reich-reverse of Bravery and Commemorative Medal of the Spanish "Blue Division" 1944.

DOE WEL EN ZIE NIET OM-Do well and do not look back-Kingdom of Holland 1806-1810-Order of the Union of Holland.

DUCE ET AUSPICE-Led and inspired-France-Order of the Holy Ghost.

E, mailed arm and sword-Estonia-Cross of Liberty.

EA-Germany-Brunswick-Ernst August Crosses I & II Class 1914.

EII-Germany-Saxe-Altenburg-Duke Ernst Medal for Bravery.

EIN GOTT EINE WAHRHEIT EIN RECHT-One God, One Truth, One Right-Germany-Oldenburg-Peter Frederick Louis Order.

EIRE-Ireland-appears on Republic of Ireland's awards.

EL-Germany-Hesse-Decoration of Honor World War I.

ELE-Germany-Hesse-Decoration of Honor for War Welfare Work 1915.

EN SOUVENIR DE SA COLLABORATION-TER HERINNERINGEN ZIJN MEDEWERKING-Belgium-Medal of the National Committee for Assistance and Food Supply 1914-18.

EN TEMOINAGE DE RECONNAISSANCE NATIONALE 1914-18-Belgium-King Albert Medal (Political Prisoners' Medal).

ERDELYI RESZEK...-Hungary-Medal for the Liberation of Siebenburgen (Transylvania) 1940.

ESTADOS UNIDOS DO BRASIL-United States of Brazil-Order of the Southern Cross-type II-and other Brazilian awards.

EX FLAMMIS CLARIOR-Shining brighter from the flame-Germany/Hohenlohe (breast star), type II.

F-Germany/Anhalt-Friedrich Cross 1914; Baden-War Merit Cross 1914.

FA 1914-Germany/Oldenburg-Friedrich August Cross I & II Class.

FAR-Germany/Saxony-Friedrich August Medal.

FF- (1st F reversed)-Germany/Mecklenburg-Schwerin-Friedrich Franz Cross 1914, Military Merit Cross.

FF- (1st F reversed)- Rumania-Order of Michael the Brave.

F.E.B.-Brazil-Brazilian Expeditionary Service Cross 1944.

FIDEI ET MERITO-Faith and Merit-Italy-Sicily-Order of St Ferdinand.

FIDEI ET VIRTUTI-Faith and Virtue-Papal States-Mentana Cross 1867.

FIDELITAS-Fidelity-Germany-Baden-House Order of Fidelity.

FIDELITE DEVOUEMENT-Fidelity and devotion-France-Order of the Cross of Fidelity-Louis XVIII.

FIDELITER ET CONSTANTER-Fidelity and constancy-Germany/Saxon Duchies-Saxe-Ernestine House Order.

FIDELITER SINE TIMORE-Fidelity without fear-Germany/Lippe-Order of Leopold.

FJ-Austria-appears on the obverse of the Franz Joseph Order, the Crosses of Merit, and the Iron Merit Crosses.

FOR AEDEL DAAD-Heroic Deeds-Denmark-Lifesaving Medal.

FOR BRAVERY IN THE FIELD-Great Britain-Military Medal-Army-(reverse).

FJ W-Austria-obverse of the War with Denmark Medal 1864.

FORCA AERA BRASILILEIRA-Brazil-Brazilian Air Force South Atlantic Campaign Medal 1942-45.

FORCA NAVAL DO NORDESTE 1942 1945-Brazil-reverse of Medal for the Northeast Naval Force 1942-45.

FORCA NAVAL DO SUL-Brazil-reverse of Medal for the Southern Naval Force 1942-45.

FOR CONSPICUOUS GALLANTRY-Great Britain-Conspicuous Gallantry Medal-Royal Navy, and Royal Air Force.

FOR COURAGE-Great Britain-Distinguished Flying Medal-Royal Air Force (reverse).

FOR DELTAGELSE I KRIGEN 1848-1850-Denmark-War Medal 1848-1850. Same with date 1864; same with dates 1848-1850 & 1864.

FOR DELTAGELSE I ALLIERT KRIGSTJENESTE 1940-45-For participation in the Allied war service-Denmark-reverse of King Christian X's Medal for War Participation 1940-1945.

FOR DISTINGUISHED CONDUCT IN THE FIELD-Great Britain-Distinguished Conduct Medal-Army-reverse.

FOR DISTINGUISHED SERVICE-Great Britain-Distinguished Service Medal (Royal Navy-reverse-with crown above inscription);Indian Distinguished Service Medal-without crown above inscription.

FOR DISTINGUISHED SERVICE-U.S.A.-Distinguished Service Medal-Army.

FOR EDAL DAD-For heroic deeds-Norway-Medal for Heroic Deeds.

FOR FAITHFUL SERVICE-Great Britain-Imperial Service Order and Medal.

FOR GALLANTRY-Great Britain-George Cross-obverse.

FOR GALLANTRY-Philippines-Distinguished Conduct Star.

FOR GALLANTRY IN SAVING LIFE ON LAND or AT SEA-Great Britain-Albert Medal.

FOR GOD AND THE EMPIRE-Great Britain-British Empire Order.

FOR GOD TJENESTE-For Good Service-Denmark-Good Service Medals for the Army, Navy and Police.

FOR MILITARY MERIT-U.S.A.-Purple Heart; Aerial Achievement Medal; Air Force, Army, Navy Commendation Medals.

FOR PUBLIC SERVICE IN INDIA-Great Britain-Kaisar-I-Hind Medal.

FOR SERVICE-U.S.A.-appears on the reverse of most campaign and service medals of the United States Armed Forces.

FORSAN VICTI NUNQUAM SERVI-Vanquished perhaps, but never enslaved-Belgium-reverse of the Medaille des Refractaires-Medal for those who refused and escaped from German forced military and labor service in World War II.

FORTIENT-Merit-Denmark-The Medal of Merit (reverse).

FOR VALOUR-Great Britain-Victoria Cross.

FORTITUDINI-For Bravery-appears on the obverse of the Austrian Maria Theresa Order, and the reverse of Austrian bravery medals of the Emperor Charles.

FORTUDINI, VIRTUTI, ET PERSEVERANTIAE-Bravery, Virtue, and Perseverance-Austria-Honor Medal for 25 Years Service in the Fire and Lifesaving Services.

FORTUDO, CARITAS, ABNEGATO-Fortitude, Charity and Abnegation-Spain-Order of Charity.

FRAUEN-VERDIENST-IM-KRIEGE-Germany/Saxe-Weimar-Eisenach-Decoration of Merit for Women.

FREDERIK DEN SIETTE DANMARKS OG NORGES KONGE-Denmark-Frederick VI King of Denmark and Norway.

FREEDOM-U.S.A.-Medal of Freedom (1945).

FREIE UND HANSESTADT HAMBURG-FÜR RETTUNG AUS GEFAHR-Germany/Hamburg-Lifesaving Medal 1918-1934.

FUER VERDIENST-Germany/Saxe-Coburg-Gotha-Carl Eduard Medal (oval), Decoration of Merit in the Homeland.

FUER VERDIENSTE UM DAS ROTHE KREUZ-Germany/Prussia-Red Cross Medal.

FÜR AUFOPFERNDE DIENSTE IM KRIEGE-Germany/Brunswick-War Merit Cross for Women World War I.

FÜR AUSZEICHNUNG IM KRIEGE-Germany/Lippe-War Merit Cross World War I.

FÜR BADENS EHRE-For Baden's Honor-Germany-Baden-Military Order of Karl Friedrich.

FÜR DIE HEIMAT-Austria-World War II Commemorative Cross (unofficial).

FÜR EHRE UND WAHRHEIT-For Honor and truth-Germany-Baden-Order of the Zaharingen Lion (breast star).

FÜR HEIMAT VERDIENST-Germany/Saxe-Weimar-Eisenach-Cross of Merit for Homeland Service 1914-18.

FÜR HELDEN MUTIGE TAT-Germany/Lippe-War Cross of Honor for Heroic Deeds 1914.

FÜR KRIEGSFURSORGE-Germany/Hesse-Decoration of Honor for War Work.

FÜR KRIEGS-HILFDIENST-Germany/Prussia-War Aid Service Cross 1915.

FÜR KRIEGS VERDIENST 1939-For war merit-Germany/III Reich-reverse of the War Merit Medal 1939.

FÜR MILITAIR-VERDIENST-Germany/Schaumburg-Lippe-Military Merit Medal World War I.

FÜR OSTERREICH-Austria-World War I Commemorative Medal.

FÜR RETTUNG-Germany-for lifesaving-various lifesaving medals of the German states.

FÜR RETTUNG AUS GEFAHR-For lifesaving with risk to oneself-Germany-various lifesaving medals.

FÜR TAPFERKEIT-For Bravery-Germany -appears on the reverse of some of the bravery medals of its pre-1919 states.

FÜR TAPFEKEIT UND TREUE-Germany/Saxe-Weimar-Eisenach-General Honor Decoration World War I.

FÜR TREUE DIENST-Germany/Reuss-Service Cross.

FÜR TREUE DIENSTE IM WELTKRIEGE-Germany/-Oldenburg-War Merit Medal World War I.

FÜR TREUE DIENSTE 1914-Germany/Schaumburg-Lippe-Faithful Service Cross World War I.

FÜR TREUE UND VERDIENST-For loyalty and merit-Germany/Lippe-Honor Cross of the House Order of Lippe; Germany/Prussia-Princely Hohenzollern Order.

FÜR TREUES WIRKEN IN EISERNER ZEIT 1914-Germany/Reuss-Devoted War Service Medal.

FÜR VERDIENST-For Merit-Germany-appears on the reverse of various awards of the German states.

FÜR VERDIENST IM KRIEGE 1914-German/Commemorative Crosses (reverse) for Bremen, Hamburg and Lubeck.

FÜR VERDIENST UM DIE KUNST-Germany/Oldenburg-For Merit in the Arts-1878-1918.

FÜR VERDIENST UND TREUE-For Merit and Loyalty - Germany/ Saxony - Civil Merit Order (to Saxons).

FÜR VERDIENSTE IM KRIEGE-Germany/Anhalt-Friedrich Cross 1914.

FÜR VERDIENSTE UM DAS ROTE KREUZ-Germany/Wurttemberg-Karl Olga Medal.

FÜR VIERZIG JAHRIGE TREUE DIENSTE-Austria-Republic-1927 & 1934-reverse 40 Year Loyal Service Medal.

FÜR WERKE DER KRIEGSHILFE 1917-Germany/Mecklenberg-Strelitz-Adolf-Friedrich Cross.

156

FURCHTLOS UND TREU-Fearless and loyal-Germany/Wurttemberg-Order of the Crown; Order of Military Merit.

FWIII-Germany-Prussia-cipher of Friedrich Wilhelm III-appears on the General Honor Decoration among other medals.

GEORGIVS.V.D.G.BRITT.OMN.REX.ET.INDIAE.IMP.-Great Britain-George V-By the Grace of God-King of All Britain and Emperor of India-obverse of many British medals of George V (1911-1936).

GERECHTKEIT IST MACHT-Justice is Power-Germany/Baden-Order of Berthold (breast star).

GOTT EHRE VATERLAND-God, honor, fatherland-Germany/Hesse-Order of Ludwig (breast star; reverse of badge).

GOTT MIT UNS-God with us-Germany/Prussia-Merit Order of the Prussian Crown; Order of the Crown.

GRANDE GUERRE 1914-1918-France-Great War (World War I) Commemorative Medal.

GRATI PRINCEPS ET PATRIA-Gratitude of the Ruler and Nation-Austria-Army Cross 1813-14-also known as the Cannon Cross.

GRI VI-Great Britain-obverse of World War II Service Stars

GUD OG KONGEN-God and the King-Denmark-Order of the Dannebrog.

GUERRA POR LA LIBERACION Y UNIDAD DE ESPAÑA 17 JULIO 1936-Italy-Campaign Medal for the Spanish Civil War.

GUERRA POR LA VNIDAD ESPANOLA (obverse) VOLVNTARIOS DE GUERRA-Italy-Volunteers' Medal for the Spanish Civil War.

GUSTAF DEN III INSTIFT MCCCLXXII-Gustav III instituted 1772-Sweden-Order of Vasa.

HEAVEN'S LIGHT OUR GUIDE-Great Britain-Order of the Star of India.

HONI SOIT QUI MAL Y PENSE-Evil be to him who evils thinks-Great Britain-Order of the Garter.

HR-Hungary-War Invalid badge-1931.

ICH DIEN-I serve-Great Britain-Order of the Bath-military.

I.H.S. (In Hoc Signo)-In this sign-Sweden-Order of the Seraphim.

I.H.S.V. (In Hoc Signo Vinces)-In this sign we conquer-Italy-Parma-Order of Constantine.

IM MEMORIAM 1941-45-Yugoslavia-Royal Yugoslav Commemorative War Cross.

IMMOTA FIDES-Steadfast and faithful-Germany-Brunswick-Order of Henry the Lion (breast star).

IMPERATRICIS AUSPICIIS-Under the protection of the Empress-Great Britain-Order of the Indian Empire.

IN ACTION FAITHFUL AND IN HONOUR CLEAR-Great Britain-Companion of Honor.

157

INDIA-Great Britain-Indian Mutiny Medal 1857; India General Service Medal 1895-1902 and 1936-39.

IN FIDE SALUS-In trust salvation-Rumania-Order of the Star.

INGENIO ET ARTI-Denmark-Medal for Artists and Scholars (reverse).

IN HOC SIGNO VINCES-In this sign we conquer-Italy-Sicily-Order of St George of the Reunion.

INITIATIEF MOED VOLHARDING-Initiative, Courage, Perseverance-Netherlands-Flying Cross 1941.

IN JURE MERITA-For legal merit-Spain-Order of St Raymond.

IN MEMORIAM 1848-1918-Austria-Franz Joseph Memorial Cross.

IN SANGUINE FOEDUS-Joined in blood-Italy-Sicily-Order of St Januarius.

IN SENIO-Among six-Germany-Hohenlohe-Order of the Phoenix (breast star), type I.

INSTRUCAO PUBLICA-Public Instruction-Portugal-Order of Public Instruction.

INTEGRITATI ET MERITO-Integrity and Merit-Austria-Order of Leopold.

ISABELLA II REINA DE ESPANA-Isabella II Queen of Spain-Spain-Order of Isabella II.

ISANMAA-The fatherland-Finland-Continuation War Medal 1941-1945.

ISANMAAN PUOLESTA-For the fatherland.-Finland-Liberty Cross Order-breast star.

ISANMAAN HYVAKSI-For the good of the nation-Finland-White Rose Order-breast star.

JE MAINTIENDRAI-I shall withstand-Luxembourg-Order of the Golden Lion of Nassau-breast star;Order of the Oaken Crown-breast star; Order of the Resistance.

JE MAINTIENDRAI-I shall withstand-Netherlands-Order of Orange-Nassau; House Order of Orange.

K-Austria-appears on the Kaiser Karl Gold and Large Silver Bravery Medals of World War I-signifies an officer's award of what had been an enlisted men's medal.

KONIGGRATZ DEN 3 JULI 1866-Germany-Prussia-Cross for the battle of Koniggratz-War with Austria 1866.

KRIEGS VERDIENST-For War Merit-Germany-various medals of the German states.

KUNNIA ISANMAA-Honor, fatherland-Finland-reverse of the Commemorative Medal of the Winter War 1939-40.

KWH II - SEINEN TAPFEREN HESSEN 1821-Germany/Hesse-Kassel-Campaign Medal for 1814-1815.

LAESO MILITI-Austria-Wounded and Injured Medal-World War I.
LA FRANCE A SES LIBERATEURS-France-Medal of Liberated France 1945.
LUD(OVICIUS) M(AGNUS) INST(ITUIT) 1693-Instituted by Louis the Great (Louis XIV) 1693-France-Order of St Louis.
L'UNION FAIT LA FORCE-In Unity There is Strength-Belgium-Orders of Leopold, Leopold II; many Belgian medals up to 1951.
LITERIS ET ARTIBUS-Letters and Arts-Austria-Order of Arts and Letters.
LUNGA NAVIGAZIONE AEREA-Italy-Airforce Long Service Medal.

M-Rumania-Order of Michael the Brave; Order of Agricultural Merit.
MARINHA DO BRASIL-Brazil-Naval Cross for Bravery 1943.
MEDAILLE COLONIALE-France reverse of the Colonial Medal.
MEDAILLE COMMEMORATIVE DE LA GUERRE - HERINNERINGSMEDAILLE VAN DEN OORLOG - Belgium - World War II Commemorative Medal-in French/Flemish-1940-45.
MEDAILLE D'OUTRE-MER-France-Overseas Service Medal.
MEIN TREUEN VOLKE VON TIROL 1866-My loyal people of the Tirol 1866-Austria-Commemorative Medal of the Tirol 1866.
MERENTI-Merit-Germany-Bavaria-Order of Military Merit.
MERIT/FOR DISTINGUISHED SERVICE-Philippines-Distinguished Service Star-obverse/reverse.
MERITO AERONAUTICO-Brazil-Aeronautical Merit Order.
MERITO AGRICOLA-Agricultural Merit-Portugal-Agricultural Merit Order.
MERITO AGRICOLA-Agricultural Merit-Spain-Agricultural Merit Order.
MERITO CIVILE E MILITARE-Civil and Military Merit-San Marino-Order of San Marino.
MERITO CIVILI TEMPORE BELLI MCMXV-Civil Merit in Time of War-Austria-War Cross for Civil Merit-1915.
MERITO INDUSTRIAL-Industrial Merit-Portugal-Order of Industrial Merit.
MERITO MILITAR-Military merit-Brazil-Military Merit Order.
MERITO MILITAR-Military merit-Mexico-Military Merit Order.
MERITO MILITARE-Military Merit-Italy-Tuscany-Order of Military Merit.
MERITO NAVAL-Brazil-Naval Merit Order.
MERITO POSTAL-Postal Merit-Spain-Postal Merit Order.
MILITANTIBUS A LATERE MEO, 1916-Austria-Franz Joseph Cross 1916.
MIL. ORD. EQUITUM MELIT BENE MERENTI-Military Order of the Knights of Malta for the well deserving-Malta-Sovereign Military Order.

M. THERESIA PARENTIS GRATIAM PRENNEM VOLUTI-Maria Theresa wishes to give thanks to her parents-Austria-Order of Elizabeth Theresa.

MÜNCHEN 1923-1933 9 Nov.-Munich 1923-1933-Germany-III Reich-Blood Order Commemorative Medal.

NA FORSA COSANTA-The Defence Forces-Ireland-Emergency Service Medal-1939-1846.

NAPOLEON III EMPEREUR-France-Emperor Napoleon III (1852-1870)-obverse of several medals including Italian campaigns 1859; China 1860; Mexico 1862-63; and some lifesaving medals.

NA SEIRBHISE REAMHCURAIM IN AGHAIDH AER-RUATHAR-Air Raid Precautions Organization-Ireland-Emergency Service Medal 1939-1946.

NEC ASPERA TERRENT-Nor do difficulties daunt-Germany-Hannover-Royal Guelphic Order.

NEMO ME IMPUNE LACESSIT-No man attacks me with impunity-Great Britain-Order of St Patrick.

NESCIT OCCASUM-It never sets-Sweden-Order of the North Star-badge.

NIHIL SINE DEO-Nothing without God-Rumania-House Order of Hohenzollen.

NUNQUAM RETRORSUM-Never Look Back-Germany-Hannover-Order of St George.

OCTO LUSTRA-Austria-40 Years Service in the Landwehr.

OJCZ ZA ZNE I. NAROD-For country and people-Poland-Order of the White Eagle-breast star-type II.

ORDEM NACIONAL DO MERITO-Brazil-National Order of Merit.

PADROEIRA DO REINO-Patroness of the kingdom-Portugal-Order of Villa Vicosa.

PARTEVIJU-For the nation-Latvia-Order of the Three Stars.

PATRIA GRATA-Thanks of the Fatherland-Belgium-reverse of National Gratitude Medals 1940-45.

PATRIA NON IMMEMOR-The fatherland is not forgetful-France-reverse of the Medal of the French Resistance 1943.

PATRIAE AC HVMANITI-Fatherland and Humanity-Austria-Red Cross awards 1914-1923.

PATRIAM SERVANDO VICTORIAM TULIT-By serving the fatherland he brought victory-France-reverse of the Order of the Liberation 1940.

PATRIOTES PROSCRIT-France-Medal for Outlawed Patriots 1954.

PAUPERUM SOLATIO-Comfort for the poor-Portugal-Order of St Isabella.

PENTRU AERONAUTICA-Rumania-Air Force Bravery Medal.

PENTRU MARINA-Rumania-Naval Bravery Medal.

PER ASPERA AD ASTRA-By striving to the stars-Germany-Mecklenberg-Schwerin-Order of the Wendish Crown.

PER LA PACE (reverses SINAI, LIBANO, UNIFIL)-Italy-Campaign Decoration for peacekeeping with the United Nations.

PER L'ITALIA OR E SEMPRE-Italy-Fascist Party Loyalty Medal.

PETRUS I BRASILIAE IMPERATOR-Pedro I Emperor of Brazil-Order of the Southern Cross-type I.

PIIS MERITIS-Piety and Merit-Austria-Cross for Military Chaplains.

POGLAVNIK ANTE PAVELIC-Leader Ante Pavelic-Croatia-appears on the obverse of bravery medals of World War II.

POLONIA RESTITUTA-Poland restored-Poland-Order of Polonia Restituta.

POUR LE MÉRITE-For Merit-Germany/Prussia-The Pour Le Mérite.

PRAEMIANDO INCITAT-Encourage by reward-Russia-Order of St Stanislaus-breast star.

PRAVDA VITEZI 1939-Truth prevails-Czechoslovakia-Bravery Medal 1939.

PREMIO A LA CONSTANCIA MILITAR-Reward for military constancy-Spain-Order of St Hermengildo.

PRIZNANJI DOMOVINE-The Nation's Gratitude-Croatia-reverse of the Wounded Medal 1943.

PRIN NOI INSINE-By ourselves-Rumania-Order of the Crown.

PRIN STATORNICE LA ISBINDA-Through perseverance success-Rumania-Order of Carol I.

PRINCEPS ET PATRIA-Prince and fatherland-Monaco-Order of St Charles.

PRO BENIGNITATE HUMANA-Finland-reverse of the Medal for Humanitarian Work 1945.

PRO DANIA 1940-45-For Denmark-reverse of King Christian X's Liberation Commemorative Medal-also known as the Medal of Liberty or the Pro Dania Medal.

PRO DEO ET PATRIA-For God and Fatherland-Hungary-reverse of the Commemorative Medals for World War I-helmet for military.

PRO FIDE PRINCIPE ET PATRIA FORTITER PVGNANTI-Austria-Defense of Tyrol-1796.

PRO FIDE REGE ET LEGE-For faith, king and law-Russia-Order of the White Eagle-breast star.

PRO FINLANDIA-For Finland-Finland-reverses of the V Class of the Order of Lion, and the Pro Finlandia Medal-1942.

PRO PATRIA ET VICTORIA-For fatherland and victory-Belgium-Colonial Service Medal 1940-45.

PRO RENOVATA PATRIA-For the reborn country-Italy-Sicily-Royal Order of the Two Sicilies.

PROVIDENTIAE MEMOR-Remembering providence-Germany-Saxony-Order of the Rue Crown.
PRO VIRTUTE BELLICA-For merit in war-France-Order of Military Merit.
PROXIMA SOLI MDCCCLV-Near to the Sun 1855-Italy-Modena-Order of the Eagle of Este.
PUBLICUM MERITORUM PRAEMIUM-Reward for Public Service-Austro-Hungarian Order of St Stephen.

QUINQUE LUSTRA-Austria-25 Years Service in the Landwehr.

R-Luxembourg-Order of the Resistance.
RAINIER GRIMALDI PRINCE OF MONACO-Prince Rainier Grimaldi of Monaco-Monaco-Order of Grimaldi.
RANNA CABHAIR DEONTACA CUMANN CROISE NA H-EIRANN-First Aid Division,Irish Red Cross-Ireland-Emergency Service Medal 1939-1946.
RSAPLATA MUNCII PENTRU INVATAMANT-Rumania-Merit Medal for Public Education.
RECOMPENSA A LA CONSTANCIA EN EL SERVICIO MILITAR-Reward for constancy in military service-Mexico-Military Long Service cross.
RECONNAISSANCE FRANCAISE-France-Medal of Gratitude-both World Wars:
Type I-obverse-female figure supporting a soldier-World War I.
Type II-obverse-female figure holding palm branch-World War II and later.
REISE S.M. SCHIFF KAISERIN ELIZABETH-Journey of H.M. Ship Empress Elizabeth-Austria-Commemorative Medal of the Cruiser Elizabeth's voyage to the Far east 1892-1893.
RELIGION INDEPENDENCIA UNION-Religion, Independence, Union-Mexico-Order of Guadalupe-obverse of badge.
RELINQUO VOS LIBEROS ABUTROQUE HOMINE-Relinquish your liberties to no man-San Marino-Order of San Marino-breast star.
RESISTERE-Belgium-reverse of the Armed Resistance Medal 1940-45.
RESISTERUNT-They resisted-Belgium-reverse of the Civil Resistance Medal 1940-45.
REWARD OF GALLANTRY or VALOR-Great Britain-Indian Order of Merit-military.

SAECULO NON INSTANTE FUNDAVIT-A people is not established in an instant-Slovakia-Order of Prince Pribina.
SALUS ET GLORIA-Health and glory-Austria-Order of the Starry Cross.
SANGUE DO BRASIL-Blood of Brazil-Brazil-Wound Medal 1945.

SANT AGATA PROTETTRICE-St Agatha Protectoress-San Marino-Order of St Agatha.

SAYO, GAMBELLA, ASOSA-Belgium-reverse of the Abyssinian Campaign Medal 1941.

SCIENCIAS, LETRAS, E ARTES-Sciences, letters, and arts-Portugal-Order of St James of the Sword.

SEIRBHIS ALTRANAIS AN AIRM-The Army Nursing Service-Ireland-Emergency Service Medal 1939-1946.

SERVICIU CREDINCIOS-Rumania-Faithful Service Medal.

SERVICOS DE GUERRA-Brazil-Naval War Services medal 1943.

SERVICOS RELEVANTES-Brazil-Naval Distinguished Service Medal 1943.

SIBI BENEFACIT QUI BENEFACIT AMICO-Netherlands-Medal of National Gratitude World War II.

SI DEUS NOBISCUM QUIS CONTRA NOS-If God is with us who can be against us?-Germany-Hesse-Order of Philip.

SI DEUS PRO NOBIS QUIS CONTRA NOS 1922-If God is with us who can be against us 1922-Hungary-Order of Merit (reverse of badges).

SIGNORE BENEDITE L'ITALIA-Italy-Medal for Military Chaplains World War II.

SIGNUM LAUDIS-Sign of praise-Austria and Hungary-Military Merit Medal.

SIGNUM MEMORIAE-Austria-50th Jubilee Year of Emperor Franz Joseph 1898.

SINCERE ET CONSTANTER-Honesty and Constancy-Prussia-Red Eagle Order (breast stars and grand cross badge).

SLOVENSKE NARODNE POVSTANIE 29.VIII 1944-Czechoslovakia National Uprising Commemorative Medal 1945.

SOUTH AFRICA-Great Britain-South Africa 1834-1853; 1877-1879; Queen's South Africa Medal 1899-1902; King's South Africa Medal 1901-1902.

SUMMO IN PERICULO FAUTPRIBUS ADIUTORIBUS-Commemorating the defenders and helpers of Finland in her greatest danger-Finland-reverse of the Commemorative Medal of the Winter War 1939-40, as awarded to foreign citizens.

SUOMI-the Finnish word for Finland.

SUSCIPERE ET FINIRE-To undertake and accomplish-Germany-Hannover-Order of Ernst August.

SUUM CUIQUE-To each his own-German-Prussia-Order of the Black Eagle (breast star).

SVERIGE-Sweden-found on obverse of Swedish medals.

TALENT DE BIEN FAIRE-Talent to do things well-Portugal-Order of Prince Henry the Navigator.

THEÂTRES D'OPÉRATIONS EXTERIEURS-France-Croix de Guerre (War Cross) for overseas operations (North Africa; Central Africa and the Far East.)

THE CONGRESS TO-U.S.A.-Medal of Honor-Army-reverse 1904 style.

TOLDI MIKLOS-Hungary-Toldi Miklos Commemorative Medal 1936.

TONKIN CHINE ANNAM 1883-1885-France-Medal for Indo-China (army issue-six campaigns; navy issue-seven campaigns.)

TRAVAIL ET PROGRES-Labor and Progress-Belgium-Order of the African Star; Royal Order of the Lion of the Congo; on various medals.

TRECEREA DUNAREI-Rumania-Trans- Danube Cross 1877-1878

TRIA JUNCTA IN UNO-Three united in one-Great Britain-Order of the Bath-military and civil.

TREUE DIENSTE BEI DER FAHNE-Germany/Prussia-Long Service Medals.

TREUE DIENSTE BEI DER FAHNE - DIENSTAUSZEICHNUNG III KLASSE (IX on a shield-reverse)-Germany/Bavaria-Long Service medal III Class for IX Years.

TREUEN KRIEGERN 1866-Germany/Prussia-Austrian War Cross 1866.

TROUW AA KONINGEN EN VADERLAND-Netherlands-Bronze Cross.

TROUW TOT IN DEN DOOD-Netherlands-Resistance Cross World War II.

26u CATHLAN-26th Battalion-Ireland-Emergency Service Medal 1939-1946.

UBIQUE PATRIAE MEMOR-Always mindful of the fatherland-Brazil-Order of Rio Branco.

UBIQUE SIMILIS-Everywhere the same-Italy-Tuscany-Order of St Joseph.

UNEF-United Nations-United Nations Emergency Force.

URHEUDESTA FOR TAPPERHET-For bravery, in Finnish & Swedish-Finland-Bravery medals.

UZ NARSUMA-For valor-Lithuania-Orderof the Cross of Vytis.

VALOR-U.S.A.-Medal of Honor-Army and Air Force.

VALEUR ET DISCIPLINE-Valor and discipline-France-Medaille Militaire (Military Medal).

VALOR LEALDADE E MERITO-Valor, loyalty and merit-Portugal-Order ofthe Tower and Sword.

VERDIENST UM DEN STAAT-Germany/Prussia-General Honor Medal (FWIII & WII).

VERNI SEBI SVORNE NAPRED-Slovakia-Order of the Slovak Cross.

VICTORIA-Great Britain-Royal Victorian Order.

VICTORIA REGINA-Great Britain-Queen Victoria-on the obverse of many British medals 19th century.

VIETNAM-Australia and New Zealand-Vietnam Service Medal.
VIGILANDO ASCENDDIMUS (obverse) - Germany/Saxe-Weimar-Eisenach-Veterans' Merit Cross 1909-1918.
VINCERE-Italy-Medal for the French Campaign 1940.
VIRIBUS UNITIS-with united forces-Austria-Order of Franz Joseph.
VIRTUTE-Virtue-Luxembourg-Order of Adolph of Nassau.
VIRTUTE IN BELLO-Virtue in war-Germany/Saxony-Order of St Henry.
VIRTUTE ET FIDELITATE-Virtue and fidelity-Germany/Hesse-Order of the Golden Lion.
VIRTUTE MILITARA-Military Virtue-Rumania- Military Bravery Medal.
VIRTUTI-Virtue-Germany/Hesse-Order of Military Merit.
VIRTUTI ET MERITO-Virtue and Merit-Spain-Order of Charles III.
VIRTUTI MILITARI-Military virtue-Poland-Order of Virtuti Militari.
VIRTUTI PRO PATRIA-Virtue for the Fatherland-Germany-Bavaria-Military Order of Max Joseph.
VIRTUTIS ET AUDACIAE MONUMENTUM ET PRAEMIUM-Award for Bravery and Audacity-U.S.A.-Certficate of Merit Medal.
VIRTUS ET HONOS-Virtue and Honor-Germany-Bavaria-Order of the Crown.
VIRTUS NOBILITAT-Virtue enobles-Netherlands-Order of the Lion.
VITEZSEGERT-Hungary-reverse of the Bravery Medals 1939.
VITT. EM. III. RE.D'ITALIA.IMP.DI.ETIOPIA-Victor Emmanuel III King of Italy and Emperor of Ethiopia-Italy-appears on the obverse of several Italian medals.
VON FELS ZUM MEER-From the rock to the sea-Germany-Prussia-Royal Hohenzollern Order.
VOOR MOED BELIED TROUW-For valor, dedication, and loyalty-Netherlands-Military Order of William.
VOOR KRIJSVERRICHTINGEN-Netherlands-War Commemorative Cross 1945.
VOOR VERDIENSTE-Netherlands-Merit Cross World War II.

W FJ-Prussia-obverse of the War with Denmark Medal 1864.
WINTERSCHLACHT IM OSTEN 1941-42-Winter campaign in the East-Germany-III Reich-reverse of the Eastern Front Medal 1941-42.

X-Austria-10 Year long service cross.
X-Poland-10 year long service medal.
XII-Austria-12 year long service cross.
XV-German-appears on 15 year long service crosses of various states.
XVI-Italy-Long Service Cross.
XX-Germany-Prussia-Landwehr (Reserve) 20 year service cross.
XX-Poland-20 year long service medal.
XXIV-Austria 24 year long service cross.

XXV-Germany-appears on various 25 year long service crosses.
XXXX ANNORUM-Austria-40 Year Faithful Service Medal-1898.

YSER-Belgium-Yser Medal and Cross for battle in 1914.

ZA BOHA, ZA NAROD-For God and the people-Slovakia-Medal for the Suppression of the Rebellion.
ZA CHRABROST-For Bravery-Czechoslovakia-Bravery Medal 1939.
ZA DOM SPREMNI-Ready to defend the fatherland-Croatia-Order of the Iron Trefoil.
ZA HRABROST-For Bravery-Croatia-Bravery Medal World War II.
ZA OBRANU SLOVENSKA V MARCI 1939-Slovakia-Medal for the Defense of Slovakia. (Issued for the "independence" of Slovakia.)
ZA ODRE, NYSE, BALTYK-Poland for the Oder, Neisse and Baltic Campaigns 1945.
ZA POLSKE WOLNOSC I LUD-Poland-Partisan Cross World War II.
ZA SVOBODU CESKOSLOVENSKA-For the freedom of Czechoslovakia-Military Order of Freedom 1946.
ZA VERNOST 1939-45-For Loyalty-Czechoslovakia-Commemorative Medal of the Second National Revolt 1946.
ZA VITEZSTYI-Czechoslovakia-Military Order of the White Lion 1945.
ZA WARSAWE-Poland-Medal for Warsaw.
ZA ZASLUGE 10 IV 1942-For Merit 10 April 1942-Croatia-Order of Merit.
ZA ZASLUHY-For Merit-Czechoslovakia-Military Merit Medal 1943.
ZA ZA'SLUHY NARODNI GARDA-Merit in the National Guard-Czechslovakia-National Guard Decoration-also known as the Order of Charles IV.
ZASLUZONYM NA POLU CHWALY-Poland-Medal for Merit on the Field of Glory.
ZWYCIESTWO I WOLNOSC-Poland-Victory medal World War II.

2. The Cyrillic Alphabet - this covers the countries that use or used the Cyrillic Alphabet, principally Russia, and related Slavic countries.

The Cyrillic alphabet, as used by Bulgaria, Montenegro, Russia, and Serbia appears to be very confusing to the user of the Roman alphabet. Although many letters are the same in both alphabets there are some very common points of confusion.
"C" what appears to be a "C" is in reality an "S".
"P" what appears to be a "P" is in reality an "R".
"B" what appears to be a "B" is in reality a "V".

"H" what appears to be an "H" is in reality an "N".
"3" what appears to be a "3" is in reality a "Z".
"y" what appears to be a "y" is in reality an "oo".
"E" has the sound of "yeh".
"X" is pronounced like a hard "ch" as in the Scottish Loch, or perhaps easier to imagine, the sound made clearing your throat.

Thus, the letters CCCP really stand for SSSR, the initials of the Russian words for Union of Soviet Socialist Republics. Obviously the Russian word HOBOE is not what it appears, but rather the word meaning new. The above is intended only to make the task of deciphering the words on the awards of the countries involved. Russian speakers will pardon me for the oversimplification displayed.

If you can learn the basic alphabet then you can look up words in a dictionary.

Below appears the Cyrillic Alphabet as modified after 1918, the English language equivalents follow each. The sound of each letter comes next.

Cyrillic Letter	Name Of Letter	Approximate English Equivalent
Аа	ah	a as in father.
Бб	beh	b as in boy
Вв	veh	v as in voice
Гг	geh	g as in go
Дд	deh	d as in dog
Ее	ye	ye in yet
Ёё	yo	yaw in yawn
Жж	zhe	zh like the "s" in measure
Зз	zeh	z as in zero
Ии	ee	i like "ee" in feel
Йй	short ee	i like "y" in boy (after vowels)
Кк	kah	c as in camp
Лл	el	l as in lamp
Мм	em	m as mother
Нн	en	n as in now
Оо	oh	o "aw" as in shawl
Пп	peh	p as in pamper
Рр	err	r as in ruby
Сс	es	s as in less
Тт	teh	t as in taste
Уу	oo	oo as in moon
Фф	ef	f as in fish

Хх	kha	kh similar to ch in Scottish "loch"
Цц	tseh	ts as in cats
Чч	cheh	ch as in chair
Шш	shah	sh as in she
Щщ	shchah	sh ch as in rash choice
Ъъ	hard sign	
Ыы	"yerry"	i as in till
Ьь	soft sign	
Ээ	reversed e	e as in let
Юю	yoo	"yu" as in yule
Яя	ya	ya as in yard

Below are Cyrillic legends and inscriptions that appear on some Russian awards, Imperial and Soviet, as well as Bulgarian, Montenegrin and Serbian items.

8.АПРЛИЯ 30.АПРИЛИЯ 1893 (8 April -30 April) 1893-Bulgaria-Prince Ferdinand's Weddding Medal.

БАМ-Soviet Russia-initials for the Baikal-Amur Railroad.

ВЪ 300 - ЛѢТІЯ ЦАРСТВОВАНІЯ ДОМА РОМАНОВЫХЪ-Imperial Russia-300th Anniversary of the Romanov Dynasty 1613-1913.

ВООРУЖЕННЫЕ СИЛЫ СССР-ЗА 20 (15, 10) ЛЕТТБ ЕЕЗУПРЕЧНОЙ СЛУЖБЫ-Soviet Russia-Armed forces of the U.S.S.R.-20 (15, 10) Years of Perfect Service.

Б.М. НПКОЛИ II ИМЕПЕАТОРЬ И САОДЕРЖЕЦЬ ВСЕРОСС-His Majesty Nicholas II-Emperor and Autocrat of all the Russias. (Found on the obverse of a number of Imperial Russian Medals.)

ВЕТЕРАН ТРДА-Soviet Russia-Veteran of Labor.

В ПАМЯАТЬ 800-ЛЕТА МОСКВЫ 1147- 1947-Soviet Russia-800th Anniversary of the City of Moscow.

В ПАМЯАТЬ 250-ЛЕТИЯ ЛЕНИНГРАДА - Soviet Russia - 250th Anniversary of the City of Leningrad.

ЗА 20 (15, 10) ЛЕТ БЕЗУПРЕЧНОЙ СЛУЖЫ МБД СССР-Soviet Russia-For 20 (15, 10) Years Perfect Service in the MVD (Ministry of the Interior) U.S.S.R.

ЗА БЕЗПОРОНЮ СЛУЖБУ ВЪ ПОЛЦІИ-Imperial Russia-Exemplary Service in the Police.

ЗА БОЕВЫЕ ЗАСЛУГ-For Battle Merit-Soviet Russia-Meritorious Service in Battle.

ЗА ВЗЯТІЕ ШТУРМОЪ АХУЛЬГО-Imperial Russia-Storming of Akhulgo 1839.

ЗА ВЗЯТІЕ БЕРЛИНА-Soviet Russia-Capture of Berlin 2 May 1945.

ЗА ВЗЯТІЕ БУДАПШТАSoviet Russia-Capture of Budapest-18 February 1945.

ЗА ВЗЯТІЕ КЕНИГСБЕРГА-Soviet Russia-Capture of Koenigsberg 10 April 1945.

ЗА ЗАСЛУГА-For Merit-Bulgaria-Medals for Merit.

ЗА ОБОРОНУ КАВКАЗА-Soviet Russia-Defense of the Causcaus, World War II.

ЗА ОБОРОНУ МОСКВЫ-Soviet Russia-Defense of Moscow, World War II.

ЗА ОБОРОНУ СЕВАСТОПОЛЯ-Soviet Russia-Defense of Sebastopol, World War II.

ЗА ОБОРОНУ СОВЕТСКОГО ЗАПОЛЯЬЯ-Soviet Russia-Defense of the Soviet Arctic, World War II.

ЗА ПОБЕДУ НАД ГЕРМАНИЕЙ-Soviet Russia-Victory over Germany, World War II.

ЗА ПОБЕДУ НАД ЯПОНИЕИ-Soviet Russia-Victory Over Japan-3 September 1945.

ЗА ПРИЗНАТЕНОСТЛЬ-Bulgaria Red Cross Medal 1915.

ЗА УСЕРДІЕ-For Zeal-Imperial Russia- Medals for Zeal

ЗА УСМИРЕНІЕ ПОЛЬСКАГО МЯТЕЖА-Imperial Russia-Suppression of the Polish Rebellion 1863-1864.

ЗА НАШУ СОВЕТКУЮ РОДИНУ-For our Soviet Motherland-Soviet Russia-found on the reverses of several World War II Campaign Medals.

ЗА ОТВАГУ-For Valor-Soviet Russia-Medal for valor 1938.

ЗА СНАСЕНЇЕ ПОГИБАВШИХЪ-For Lifesaving-Imperial Russia-Lifesaving Medal.

ЗА ТРУДОВУЮ ДОБЛЕСТЬ-For Valiant Labor-Soviet Russia.

ЗА ТРУДОВОЕ ОТЛИЧИЕ-For Distinguished Labor-Soviet Russia.

ЗА ТРУДЫ НОЕЧЕСТВО-For Labor and the Fatherland-Imperial Russia-Order of St Alexander Nevsky-breast star.

ЗА ХРАБРОСТЬ-For Bravery-Imperial Russia-Reverse of the Medals of St George.

ГВАРДИЯ-Soviet Russia-Badge of Soviet Guards Units

КАВКАЗ 1871 ГОДА-Imperial Russia-Medal for the Caucasus 1871.

КАГУЛЪ-Kagul-Imperial Russia-Victory in battle of Kagul 1770.

КИНБУРНЪ .1 КТЯБРЯ 1787-Imperial Russia-Capture of Kinburn 1 October 1787.

ЛЕНИН-Lenin-Soviet Russia-Order of Lenin.

МОНЕТНЫЙ ДВОР-House of the Mint-Soviet Russia-this appears on the reverse of a number of Soviet Russian awards; in effect the official hallmark.

МИЛАН ОБРЕНОВИЋ IV. КЊАЗ СРБСКИ-Serbia-Milan Obrenovich IV, Prince of Serbia. Apears on obverse or reverse of several Serbian medals.

МИЛОШ ОБЛИЋ-Montenegro and Serbia-Milosh Oblitch Medal.

НЕ НАМЪ, НЕ НАМЪ, А ИМЕНИ ТВОЕМУ. Not for us, Not for us, But in thy Name-Imperial Russia-Medals for the War of 1812; Liberation of the Peasants 1861.

ОДЛИЧНОМ СТРЕЛЦУ-Serbia/Yugoslavia-Marksman's Medal.

ОКТЯБРЬСКАЯ РЕВОЛЮЦЯ-October Revolution-Soviet Russia-Order of the October Revolution.

ОТЕЧЕСТВЕННАЯ ВОЙНА-Patriotic war-Soviet Russia-Order of the Patriotic War-World War II-in two classes.

ПЕТАР I КРАЉ СРБУ- Peter I King of Serbia.

PEBNOST-Merit-Serbia-Medal for Merit.

CCCP=SSSR-in English USSR-Union of Soviet Socialist Republics-found on Soviet awards.

СЛАВА-Glory-Soviet Russia-Order of Glory (three classes).

СТЕП-Literally "step"-Imperial Russia-found on the reverse of the Crosses and Medals of St George. These were "step" decorations. That is, one had to receive the 4th class before one could "step up" to or receive the 3rd class.

ТРУДОВА СЛАВА-Labor Glory-Soviet Russia-Order of Labor Glory (three classes).

3. The Greek Alphabet - Greek awards present a particular problem for the Western collector. I have indicated below some of the Greek awards that a collector is likely to come across, but this not a complete listing.

ΑΓΙΑ ΣΟΦΙΑ - ΑΓΙΑ ΟΛΓΑ-Order of Sts Sophia and Olga.

ΑΞΙΑι-Silver Cross of the National Gendarmerie.

ΑΣΤΥΝΟΜΙΑ ΠΟΛΕΩΝ-Police Merit Cross (gilt, silvered and bronze.)I

ΔΙ΄ΕΥΔΟΚΙΜΟΠ ΥΓΗΡΕΣΙΑΝ-Army Long Service Medal (gilt, silvered, and bronze medals.)

ΕΛΛΑΣ 1916-1917-War Cross (reverse).

ΕΛΛΗΝΙΚΟΣ ΕΡΥΘΡΟΣ ΣΤΑΥΡΟ-Red cross Medal for the Balkan Wars 1912-1913-bronze/namel.

ΕΟΝΙΚΗ ΑΝΤΙΣΙΣ 1941-1945-National Resistance Medal.

ΓΕΩΡΓΙΟΣ Β·ΒΑΣΙΛΕΥΕ ΤΩΝ ΕΛΛΗΝΩΝ-George II King of the Hellenes-appears on the obverse of the Army Long Service Medals.

ΙΣΧΥΕ ΜΟΥΗ ΑΓΑΤΤΗΤΟΥ ΛΑΟΥ-Order of George I.

ΚΩΝΣΤΑΤΙΝΟΣ ΒΑΙΛΕΥΣ ΤΩΝ ΕΛΛΗΝΩΝ-Constantine King of Hellenes-appears on obverse of the Balkan War Medal 1913.

ΝΑΥΤΙΚΟΝ ΑΠΟΜΑΧΙΚΟΝ ΤΑΜΕΙΟΝ-Medal of the Seaman's Pension Fund.

1940-1941 ΗΓΕΙΡΟΣ ΑΛΒΑΝΙΑ ΜΑΚΕΔΟΝΑ ΟΡΑΗ ΚΡΗΤΗ-War Medal 1940-1941-army reverse-for the Albanian, Macedonian, Thracian, and Cretan campaigns.

1941-45 Β. ΑΦΡΙΚΗ Ν. ΑΙΓΑΙΟΥ ΙΤΑΛΙΑ-War Medal 1941-1945-reverse for the Army. For campaigns in N. Africa, Aegean Islands, and Italy. (The medal is a star surmounted by a crown.)

3 ΣΕΠΤΕΜΒΡΙΟΥ 1843-Commemorative Medal of the Revolution of 1843-a cross of iron with a wreath (reverse).

4. Dated Awards - The dates may appear on the obverse or reverse.

1389-1912-13-Montenegro-Balkan Wars Campaign Medal.
1613-1913-Russia-300th Anniversary of the Romanov Dynasty.
1696-1896-Montenegro-Order of Petrovich-Njegosh.
1706-Russia-Medal for Kalish.
1709-Russia-Victory at Poltava.
1714-Russia-Battle of Gangut.
1720-Russia-Capture of Four Swedish Frigates.
1721-Russia-Peace of Nystadt.
1759-Russia-Battle of Kunersdorf (Seven Years War).
1770-Russia-Victory at Kagul; Victory at Tschesme.
1774-Russia-Turkish Peace Medal.
1787-Russia-Capture of Kinburn.
1788-Russia-Ochakov Cross and Medal.
1789-Russia-Victory over the Swedes in Finnish waters.
1790-Russia-Swedish Peace Treaty; Ismail Cross and Medal.
1791-Russia-Turkish Peace Treaty.
1794-Russia-Praga Cross and Medal.
1792-Poland-Order of Virtuti-Republic 1919.
1797-1897-Germany-Centenary of Kaiser Wilhelm I.

1803-1806-Russia-Circumnavigation of the Globe.

1804-Russia-Storming of Gandzha.

1805-Russia-To the Useful Medal; Loyal Zeal Medal.

1807-Russia-Preuschiche-Eylau Cross.

1809-Russia-Crossing the Swedish Coast; Battle of Torneo.

1810-Russia-Bazardzhik Cross and Medal.

1812-Russia-War of 1812; Chaplains' Cross for War of 1812.

1812-1912-Russia-100th Anniversary of War of 1812.

1813-Germany-Prussia-Iron Cross.

1813-Germany-Prussia-Campaign Medal 1813.

1813-14-Germany-Prussia-Campaign Medal 1813-14.

1813-14-15-Germany-Prussia-Campaign Medal 1813-15.

1813-1863-Germany-Prussia-50th Anniversary of the Battle of Leipzig.

1813-1913-Russia 100th Anniversary of the Battle of Leipzig.

1814-Germany-Prussia-Campaign Medal 1814.

1815-Germany-Prussia-Campaign Medal 1815-awarded for campaigns relating to Battle of Waterloo.

1817-1842-Russia-VI Royal Prussian Cuirassier Regimental Jubilee Medal.

1819-Russia-Polar Expedition.

1822-Greece-Medal for the National Assembly.

1826-Greece-Medal for Defense of Missolonghi.

1828-1829-Russia-Turkish War.

1830-1930-Centenary of Belgian Independence.

1831-Russia-Subjugation of Polish Rebellion; Capture of Warsaw.

1833-Russia-Mouraviev Campaign.

1835-Russia-Russo-Prussian Maneuvers.

1843-Greece-Star and Cross of the Revolution of 1843.

1847-Montenegro-Milosh Oblich Medal.

1848-Austria-Defense of the Tyrol.

1848-Great Britain-Naval General Service Medal; Military General Service Medal.

1848-1898-Austria-50th Jubilee Year Medal of Franz Joseph.

1848-1908-Austria-60th Year Jubilee Cross of Franz Joseph, and various Jubilee medals.

1849-Austria-on the reverse of the Franz Joseph Order, and the Crosses of Merit.

1849-Germany-Prussia-Hohenzollern Campaign Medal.

1849-Russia-Conquest of Transylvania.

1851-Montenegro-Milosh Oblich Medal.

1852-3-Montenegro-Orders of St Peter and Danilo.

1853-Great Britain-Medal for South African Campaigns.

1853-54-55-56-Russia-Crimean War; Chaplains' Cross for the Crimean War.

1855-1905-Russia-50th Anniversary of the Defense of Sevastopol.
1857-58-59-Russia-Conquest of Chechnya and Dagestan.
1858 (1st of May)-Montenegro-Medal for the battle of Grahovo.
1859-1864-Russia-Conquest of the Western Caucasus.
1860-1900-Montenegro-40th Anniversary of Nicholas I.
1860-1910-Montenegro-50th Anniversary of Nicholas I.
1861-Russia-Liberation of the Serfs.
1862-Montenegro-Medal for Courage.
1863-1864-Russia-Pacification of the Polish Rebellion.
1863-1895-Russia-Central Asian Campaigns.
1863-1915-1913-Greece-Order of George I.
1864-1914-Austria-reverse of Red Cross Decorations and Medals.
1864-Russia-Cross for the Caucasus.
1865-1905-Belgium-40th Anniversary of Leopold II.
1866-Austria-Defense of the Tyrol.
1866-Austria-obverse of the Prague Citizens' Medal 1866.
1866-Germany-various states' medals and crosses for the war with Austria.
1870-France-Legion of Honor-III Republic; Medaille Militaire-III Republic.
W 1870-Germany-Prussia-Iron Cross.
1870-71-France-Franco-Prussian War Commemorative Medal.
1870-71-Germany-Franco-Prussian War Commemorative Medal-in bronze (combat), and steel (non-combat); various medals and crosses from the states.
1871-Austria-reverse of the Marianer Cross.
1871-Russia-Medal for the Caucasus.
2 DECEMBER 1873-Austria-reverse of the General Campaign Medal.
1873-Russia-Khiva Campaign.
1875-1876-Russia-Conquest of Khokand.
1877-78-Bulgaria-War of Liberation Medal.
1877-1878-Russia-Turkish War.
1878-Bulgaria-Order of St Alexander.
1878-Russia-Liberation of Bulgaria.
1879-Bulgaria-Military Bravery Order and Crosses; Medal for Election of Prince Alexander I.
1881-Russia-Medal for the Storm and Siege of Gheok-Teppe; Commemorating Alexander II.
1881-1894-Commemorating Alexander III.
1883-Russia-Coronation of Alexander III.
1885-Bulgaria-Serbian War Medal.
1887-Bulgaria-Cross for Election of Ferdinand I; Military Long Service Crosses.
1887-Great Britain-Medals for Queen Victoria's 50th Jubilee Year.
1891 (2nd August)-Bulgaria-Civil Merit Order; Military Merit Order.

174

1893-Bulgaria-Prince Ferdinand's Wedding Medal.
1896-Russia-Coronation of Nicholas II.
1897-Great Britain-Medals for Queen Victoria's 60th Jubilee Year.
1897-Russia-First general Census.
1900-1901-Russia-Boxer Rebellion.
1901-Bulgaria-Commemorating the Insurrection of 1876.
1903-1909 (reverse 1931)-Greece-Medal for the Struggle for Macedonia (Republican issue.)
1903-1909 (reverse 1936) as above-Royal issue.
1904-Russia-Chemulpo Medal.
1904-1905-Russia-Russo-Japanese War.
1908-Austria-Annexation of Bosnia-Herzegovina.
1908-Bulgaria-Cross for Proclamation of the Kingdom.
1912-Montenegro-Red Cross Order.
1912-1913-Montenegro-Red Cross Order.
1912-1913-obverse; reverse 1389-Montenegro-Red Cross Medal.
1912-1913-Austria-Balkan Wars Mobilization Cross 1912-1913.
1912-1913-Bulgaria-Balkan Wars Commemorative Medal.
1912-1913-Greece-Medal for the 1st Balkan War.
1913-Montenegro-Red Cross Order.
1913-Greece-Medal for the 2nd Balkan War (reverse dates 976-1025.)
1914-Germany-Prussia-Iron Cross.
1914-Germany-sundry awards of the German States for World War I.
1914 (Aug Nov)-Great Britain-1914 Star.
1914 (reverse 1936)-Greece-Medal for North Epirus.
1914-Russia-Distinguished Services in the Mobilization.
1914-15-Great Britain-1914-15 Star.
1914-1915-France-Croix de Guerre.
1914-1916-France-Croix de Guerre.
1914-1917-France-Croix de Guerre.
1914-1918-France-Croix de Guerre.
1914-1918-Germany-Weimar Republic/Third Reich-War Honor Crosses.
1914-1916-Belgium-African Campaign Medal-World War I.
1915-Bulgaria-Military Bravery Order and Crosses.
1915-1916-Bulgaria-Military Bravery Order-pinback breast cross.
1915-1917-Bulgaria-Military Bravery Order-pinback breast cross.
1915-1918-Bulgaria-World War I Commemorative Medal
1916-Austria-reverse of the Iron Merit Crosses.
1916-Bulgaria-Red Cross decoration.
1916-1917-Greece-War Cross (with vertical sword.)
1916-1917-Greece-Military Merit Medal.
1916-18-Rumania-War Cross.

1914-1918-Many medals from various countries reflecting commemoration of World War I; especially the World War I Victory Medals.

1923-Austria-reverse of Red Cross awards.

1939-France-Croix de Guerre.

1939-Germany-III Reich-Iron Cross, War Merit Cross, War Merit Medal.

1939-Poland-Valor Cross.

1939-1945-France-Croix de Guerre.

1939-1945-Great Britain-War Medal.

1940-Greece-Distinguished Conduct Medal; War Cross; Merchant Navy Cross.

1940-1944-Greece-Navy Campaign cross.

1940-1941-Greece-Campaign Medal.

1941-Bulgaria-Military Bravery Order and Crosses.

1941-Germany-III Reich-War Order of the German Cross often referred to as the German Cross.)

1941-1945-Greece-Campaign Star; National resistance Medal.

1944-Poland-Polonia Restituta Order; Valor Cross (Communist issues).

1945-Greece-Air Force Valor Cross; Air Force Cross and Medal of Merit; Air Force Distinguished Service Medal; Air Force Convoy Escort and Army Reconnaissance Medal.

1948-Greece-Air Force Flying Cross.

1950-Greece-Distinguished Conduct Medal.

5. CIPHERS OF VARIOUS MONARCHS.

A-Belgium-Albert.

AI-Russia-Alexander I.

AII-Russia-Alexander II.

AIII-Russia-Alexander III.

C-Luxembourg-Charlotte.

EAR-Germany-Hannover-Ernst August.

EII-Russia-Catherine II (the Great).

EIIR-Elizabeth II.

ERI-Great Britain-Edward VII.

FJ-Austria-Franz Joseph.

GRI-Great Britain-George V and George VI.

GVIR-Great Britain-George VI.

"HI"-Russia-Nicholas I,

"HII"-Russia-Nicholas II.

L-Belgium-Leopold.

LII-Belgium-Leopold II.

LIII-Belgium-Leopold III.

MOIII-Serbia-Milosh Oblitch III.
MOIV-Serbia-Milosh Oblitch IV.
WI-Germany/Prussia-Wilhelm I.
WII-Germany/Prussia-Wilhelm II; Wuertemberg-Wilhelm II.
WR IV-Germany-Hannover-William IV.

6. RULERS OF GERMAN STATES-World War I

Kingdoms
Bavaria-Ludwig III
Prussia-Wilhelm II (also German Emperor)
Saxony-Friedrich August III
Wurttemberg-Wilhelm II.

Grand Duchies
Baden-Friedrich II
Hesse-Darmstadt-Ernst Ludwig
Mecklenburg-Schwerin-Friedrich Franz IV
Mecklenburg-Strelitz-Adolf Friedrich VI
Oldenburg-Friedrich August
Saxe-Weimar-Wilhelm Ernst

Duchies
Anhalt-Friedrich II
Brunswick-Ernst August
Saxe-Altenburg-Ernst II
Saxe-Coburg-Gotha-Carl Eduard
Saxe-Meiningen-Bernhard III

Principalities
Lippe-Detmold-Leopold IV
Reuss (senior line)-Heinrich XXIV
Reuss (junior line)-Heinrich XXVII
Schaumburg-Lippe-Adolf
Schwartzburg-Rudolstadt-Gunther
Schwartzburg-Sonderhausen-Gunther
Waldeck-Pyrmont-Friedrich

Single Headed Eagle. Mexico, Order of the Mexican Eagle.

Double Headed Eagle. Top left - Russia, Order of St. Stanislas, III Class (crowned eagle). Bottom right - Albania, Order of Scanderbeg, Knight (uncrowned eagle).

Lions. Top left - Belgium, Order of the Lion, Knight. Top right - Bulgaria, Civil Merit Order, Officer. Bottom left - Finland, Order of the Lion of Finland, Officer. Bottom right - Netherlands, Order of Orange-Nassau, Knight.

St. George and the Dragon. Great Britain, The George Medal.

CHAPTER VIII

RIBBON DEVICES

Among the variety of ways to identify or recognize an Order, Medal or Decoration is a device placed on the ribbon or the ribbon bar to denote some specific factor. A clear example is that of the rosette which is found on the ribbons of some awards.

A rosette on the ribbon of an Order will indicate that it is the IV Class (also known as Officer). Thus, if you have an Order from France, Belgium, or even Japan that has a rosette on the ribbon, you may presume that it is the IV Class. Some countries will use the rosette to indicate a I Class of a decoration which otherwise is identical to the II Class. The Belgian Military Cross is identical in both classes, except that the I Class has a rosette on the ribbon. The French Resistance Medal for World War II is similar.

In order to avoid making the introduction too long, I will go country by country and indicate some examples.

Austria

Crossed swords on the ribbons of various Orders and Medals to show combat or frontline service.

III Class of the Iron Crown and Franz Joseph Orders; III Class of the Military Merit Cross; Military Merit (Signum Laudis) Medals. Republic-World War I Commemorative and Tyrol Commemorative Medals.

Kleine Dekoration-the practice of wearing a miniature of a higher class of an Order on the ribbon of the lowest class to show entitlement to it. This would involve the multi class Orders, Maria Theresa, Leopold, Iron Crown, and Franz Joseph, and the Military Merit Cross.

Metal bars, singly and in multiples, horizontally on the ribbons of bravery medals during World War I indicate additional awards.

Capital "K" on the ribbon of the Kaiser Karl Golden Bravery, and Large Silver Bravery Medals to indicate an award to officers.

Belgium

Crossed swords on the ribbons on the V Class of various Orders to indicate a military or combat award, such as the Orders of the Crown, and Leopold II.

Bars, lions, red crosses on the ribbon of the World War I & II Commemorative Medals.

Palmes on the ribbons of several Orders, including Leopold I & II, and the Croix de Guerre of World Wars I & II, and the Overseas Service Croix de Guerre of 1951.

Campaign bars for Medals in both World Wars, including the Colonial Service Medal, Africa Service Medal, World War II Commemorative (Victory) Medal, Volunteers Medal for the Korean War, and the Service Medal for the Korean War.

Bulgaria

Rosettes on the ribbons of IV Classes of Orders of Military Merit, Civil Merit, and St Alexander.

Croatia

The medal of the Order of the Crown of Zvonimir can come with an oakleaf wreath on the ribbon.

Czechoslovakia

Linden leaves on the ribbons of various medals, to indicate additional awards.

Campaign bars on the Revolutionary Cross 1918, and the World War II Commemorative Medal.

Finland

The Winter War Medal for service against Soviet Russia 1941-1944 was awarded with campaign bars, and could also be found with small crossed swords on the ribbon. The Civil Defense Medal is found with the bar 1941-1944 on the ribbon.

France

Gilt palmes on the ribbons of various medals to show their class or distinction. Bronze palmes on the ribbons of Croix de Guerre to show unit awarding as well as to indicate repeat awards.

Stars on the ribbons of Croix de Guerre with similar purpose to palmes.

Rosettes on the IV Class of the Legion of Honor, and National Merit Orders, as well as the Officer grade of the various other French, and French Colonial Orders. These are used also to indicate grades of various other awards of France. Two examples would be the medals of honor of

183

the various government departments, and the Resistance Medal of World War II.

Germany

Despite the thousands of awards from Germany and its constituent states, not many had devices added to their ribbons.

BADEN-Service bars for the Field Service Medal of 1848 as follows: 1805; 1806; 1806-1807; 1807; 1809; 1809-1810; 1812; 1808-1813; 1813; 1814; 1814-1815; 1848; 1849; 1866; 1870; 1870-1871.

BAVARIA-Service bars for the Merit Cross for Health Service Volunteers 1901.
1870/71; 1914; with crown and 1914.
BRUNSWICK-Combat Decoration for the War Merit Cross II Class (Ernst August Cross) 1914.

OLDENBURG-Combat bar "VOR DEM FEINDE" for the Friedrich August Cross II Class 1914.

PRUSSIA-25 year commemorative oakleaves for Iron Cross II Class 1870; 1914 bar for the Iron Cross II Class 1870.

SAXE-COBURG-GOTHA-Commemorative bars for the oval silver medal of Duke Carl Eduard.
1914; 1914/5; 1914/6; 1914/7; 1914/8; with swords & 1914; with swords & 1914/5; with swords
& 1914/6; with swords & 1914/7; with swords and 1914-8.

EMPIRE:
Campaign bars for the Franco-Prussian War Medal 1870-1871-combat issue-several types.
Campaign bars for China 1900-1901 War Medal (Boxer Rebellion)-combat issue.
Campaign bars for the Southwest Africa Medal-combat issue.
Campaign bars for the Colonial Service Medal-combat issue.
With the exception of the bars for the first listed all the others are scarce to rare.

WEIMAR REPUBLIC
Unofficial awards of various veterans' groups. These are being mentioned as they are found frequently on mounted German groups.
German Honor Legion Medal-wreath with sword.

Kyffhauser Bund-campaign bars on oval service medal.
Marine Corps-there are campaign bars on the ribbon of the Flanders' Cross for the Marine Corps.

III REICH
1939 bar for the Iron Cross II Class 1914.
Prague Castle bar 1939 for the Sudetenland Medal 1938.
Eagle and wreath for the Police Long Service Cross.
Eagle and wreath for the Armed Forces 40 Year Long Service Cross.
Eagles for the Armed Forces Long Service Crosses and Medals.
Embroidered Gilt Metal "SS" on the SS 25 Year Long Service Decoration.
Embroidered Silver Metal "SS" on the SS 12 Year Long Service Decoration.

Great Britain

Inasmuch as most of the campaign medals of this country have had bars or clasps to commemorate some active campaign service, it is important to emphasize that with the few exceptions noted below, they were attached to the suspension of the medal itself, rather than being slid over or attached to the ribbon by prongs or being sewn on. **Those items are not included below.**

Gallantry Decorations-Bars for additional awards-in alphabetical order.
Air Force Cross; Air Force Medal;
Burma Gallantry Medal;
Conspicuous Gallantry Medal (Naval & Air);
Distinguished Conduct Medal (early ones were dated); Distinguished Flying Cross; Distinguished Flying Medal; Distinguished Service Cross; Distinguished Service Medal;
George Cross; George Medal;
Indian Police Medal;
Military Cross; Military Medal;
Queens (Kings) Fire Service Medal; Queens Gallantry Medal; Queens (Kings) Police Medal;
Victoria Cross.

Additional award bars are granted also with The Royal Red Cross.

Oakleaves
Gallantry award of the British Empire Medal.
Oakleaves
Mention in despatches. For World War I the oakleaves were worn on the Victory Medal ribbon. For later awards they were to be worn on the

ribbon of the appropriate campaign medal. For World War II they were to be worn on the ribbon of the War Medal.

Campaign Medals-Bars for campaign service.
Most bars for campaign service have been attached to the medal, and the ribbon has been threaded through the assembly. However, for economy reasons there have been some exceptions where the bar has been sewn on ribbon.

1914 Star-bar April November 1914.
1939-45 Star-bar BATTLE OF BRITAIN
Atlantic Star-bars AIR CREW EUROPE; FRANCE AND GERMANY.
Air Crew Europe Star-bars ATLANTIC; FRANCE AND GERMANY
Africa Star-bars 1 ST. ARMY; 8TH ARMY; N. AFRICA 1942-43.
Pacific Star-bar BURMA.
Burma Star-bar PACIFIC.
France and Germany Star-bar ATLANTIC.

Bars for Long Service Medals
Included are the Navy Long Service and Good Conduct-George V, and Wartime and Peacetime service bars for the Special Constabulary Medal. Territorial Decorations and Medals; Efficiency Decorations and Medals; Other Reserve Awards for the Royal Navy and Royal Air Force.

Metal rosette for the South Atlantic Medal to denote combat operations.

Greece

Campaign bars for the Balkan Wars Medals 1912-13, and 1913.
Royal Navy Campaign Cross-World War II-for each 6 months' service a small star (gilt for officers; silver for petty officers, and bronze for enlisted men) is worn on the ribbon, Medal for Outstanding Acts-1940 with bar 1940 (later discontinued).

Military Merit Medal
I Class-gilt wreath-Generals and Admirals
II Class-silver wreath-Colonels and Captains
III Class-bronze wreath-Lt Colonels; Majors; Commanders; Lt Commanders.

War Cross 1917 (copies exist)
I Class-bronze palm
II Class-bronze star

Hungary

Kleine Dekoration (see Austria and glossary)-on the lowest grade of the Orders of St Stephen, Merit and the Holy Crown.

Italy

Monarchy

Bronze Roman Sword-placed on the ribbons of the Crosses of Merit 1918-1946 to denote gallantry in action; Merito di Guerra (War Merit Cross); Croce Al Valore Militare (Military Valor Cross); Al Valore Militare (Military Valor).

Campaign bars are to be found on:
The Independence Medal 1848-1849: 1855-1856, 1859, 1860-1861, 1866, 1870.
Italo-Turkish War Medal 1911-1912: 1911, 1912.
World War I Commemorative Medal 1915-1918: 1915, 1916 1917, 1918.

Republic

Campaign bars are to be found on:
War Commemorative Medal 1940-1943: 1940, 1941, 1942, 1943.
War Commemorative Medal 1943-1945: 1943, 1944, 1945.

Japan

Rosettes are to be found on the IV class of the Orders of Golden Kite, the Rising Sun, and the Sacred Treasure. Various size rosettes are to be found on the Red Cross Medals.

Silver bars may be found on the ribbon of the Merit Medal for additional awards. For the sixth award a gold bar is exchanged for the first five.

Latvia

The medal for the 10th Anniversary of Independence comes with swords on the ribbon.

Lithuania

The Cross of Vytis may come with a small triangular device, or with oakleaves.

187

Luxemburg

Rosettes are found on the IV Class (Officer) of the Orders of Adolf, Oaken Crown and Merit. Earlier issues of the Oaken Crown IV Class have a wreath between the arms, and no rosette.

Palmes are to be found on the ribbon of the Croix de Guerre 1940.

Netherlands

Campaign bars are to be found on the following: Expedition Cross (33-copies exist); World War II Commemorative Cross (12); Cross for Order and Peace (Five-1945, 1946, 1947, 1948, 1949); Cross for Right and Freedom (Korean War); New Guinea Commemorative Cross (One-1962).

Norway

The War Cross 1940-45 may be found with a sword (for combat) on the ribbon.

Poland

The Valor Cross dated 1920 is found with bars to signify additional awards.

Portugal

The World War I Service Cross may be found with a miniature cross on the ribbon. The World War I Commemorative Medal may be found with campaign bars. The medal was struck in gilt, silver and bronze. There were two issues, with the head on the obverse looking right or left.

Rumania

Campaign bars are to be found on the 1916-1918 and the 1916-1919 Commemorative Crosses: ARDEAL, BUCURESTI, CARPATI, CERNA, DOBROGEA, DUNAREA, JIU, MARASESTI, MARASTI, OITUZ, TARGUL OCMA, TURTUCAIA, SIBERIA, ITALIA. TRADITIE. Dated bars may be found also, sometimes in combination with the others.

Campaign bars are also to be found on the Anti-Communist Campaign Medal for service in Russia 1941-1944. Klietman says that the bars appeared silver and bronze, but I have only seen the latter. The bars include: AZOV; BASARABIA; BUCOVINA; BUG; CRIMEA; DOBROGEA; DONET; MEAREA NEAGRA; NIPRU; NISTRU; and ODESSA.

Slovakia

The independence medal of 1939 has the bar JAVORINA on the ribbon.

Turkey

The Imtiaz and Liakat Medals for World War I had a bar with crossed sabres attached slipped over the ribbon.

United States of America

Gallantry Awards
Army and Air Force
Oak leaf clusters are placed on the medal ribbon to indicate additional awards.
Navy, Marine Corps and Coast Guard
Gold stars are placed on the medal ribbon to indicate additional awards.
All Branches of the Armed Forces
A "V" for Valor is placed on the ribbons of the Legion of Merit; the Bronze Star; the Army, Navy and Air Force Commendation Medals to convert these to gallantry awards.

The above does not apply to the Medal of Honor.

Distinguished Service, Meritorious Service, Commendation, and Achievement Medals
Army and Air Force
Oak leaf clusters are placed on the ribbon to indicate additional awards.
Navy, Marine Corps, and the Coast Guard
Gold stars are placed on the ribbon to indicate additional awards.

Purple Heart
Army and Air Force
Oak leaf clusters are place on the ribbon to indicate additional awards.
Navy, Marine Corps and Coast Guard
Gold stars are placed on the ribbon to indicate additional awards.

Air Medal
Army and Air Force
Oak leaf clusters are placed on the medal ribbon to indicate additional awards. Due to the multiple awards that took place, especially during the

Vietnam War, one silver oak leaf cluster replaced five bronze. For exceptionally high number of awards (the record is supposed to be 263 awards to one man) a system of Arabic numerals was employed on the medal ribbon. It should be pointed out that this was primarily a USAF matter.

Navy, Marine Corps and Coast Guard
Gold stars are placed on the ribbon to indicate additional awards.

Campaign and Service Medals
Bars
West Indies Naval Campaign Medal (Sampson Medal) - bars bearing ship's name have a brooch pin and catch on the reverse, with campaign bars on the ribbon.

Haiti 1915 USN - bar 1919-1920 used to indicate the recipient served in the later Haitian campaign.

World War I Victory Medal used as a Campaign and Service Medal.

Army campaign bars.
Defensive Sector, Cambrai, Somme, Defensive, Lys, Aisne, Montdidier-Noyon, Champagne-Marne, Aisne-Marne, Somme, Offensive, Oise-Aisne, Ypres-Lys, St Mihiel, Meuse-Argonne, and Vittorio-Veneto.

Navy service bars.
Overseas, Armed Guard, Asiatic, Atlantic Fleet, Aviation, Destroyer, Escort, Grand Fleet, Mine Laying, Mobile Battery, Mine Sweeping, Naval Battery, Patrol, Salvage, Subchaser, Submarine, Transport, West Indies, and White Sea.

Country service bars.
England, France, Italy, Russia, and Siberia.

"Maltese Cross"- for non-combatant service with the Navy and Marine Corps. (Although this device is actually a cross pattée, it has always been referred to even in official documents as a "Maltese Cross.")

"Silver citation star" - for gallantry , worn on the Victory Medal ribbon. In 1932 it was replaced by the Silver Star Medal.

American Defense Service Medal
Army and Air Corps
Bars FOREIGN SERVICE-pinned onto the ribbon.
Navy and Coast Guard
Bars FLEET; BASE; SEA - slipped over the ribbon- copies of SEA bars exist.

World War II Occupation Medals
Army and Air Force
Bars JAPAN and GERMANY - pinned onto the ribbon
Navy and Marine Corps
Bars ASIA and EUROPE -slipped over the ribbon.
Note 1. The Army and Air Force version is also found with a miniature C-54 airplane on the ribbon to indicate the recipient's participation in the Berlin Air Lift 1949. This was replaced by the Humane Action Medal (commonly referred to the "Berlin Airlift Medal" .)
Note 2. The bar KOREA sometimes found on this medal's ribbon is unofficial.

Since the American Campaign Medal, others from World War II, and later campaign and service medals have carried small bronze stars on the medal ribbon to indicate campaigns fought in, or multiple periods of service. This did not apply to the World War II Occupation Service Medals.
Arrowheads were used to signify participation in amphibious landings.

Good Conduct Medals
Army and Air Force
A system of roped knots to indicate multiple awards.
Navy
A variety of bars to indicate multiple awards. They began as clip on bars, changing to pin on, followed by slipovers. The early bars were engraved to show ship and/or station, later to be replaced by SECOND AWARD, THIRD AWARD etc.; finally by small bronze stars for each enlistment.
Marine Corps
Slipover bars engraved with number of enlistment.
Coast Guard
Slipover bars were engraved to show ship or station.

Vietnam

Campaign Star usually found with the bar 1960. It can also come with earlier dated bars, for example, 1948, for the French campaign against the Viet Minh (Viet Cong).

Austria Hungary, Military Merit Cross, III Class with "Kleine Dekoration".

Top left - Belgium, 1914-1918 War Medal with combat service bars. Top right - Germany, Brunswick Ernst-August Cross, II Class 1914 with combat bar. Bottom - Greece, Red Cross Medal with additional award stars.

Top - Italy, Turkish War Medal 1911-1912 with campaign bars. Bottom
left - Vietnam, Air Force Meritorious Service Medal with wing device.
Bottom right - Vietnam, Campaign Star with 1960 bar and pre 1960 bar.

Belgian ribbon devices. Top - Maritime Medal, World War II with crossed anchors. Bottom left - Order of Leopold II, Knight with crossed swords. Bottom right - 1914-1918 Croix de Guerre with palm and lions.

United States Navy medal group, Vietnam War era. Top left to right -
Navy Commendation Medal with combat "V", Purple Heart with gold star,
National Defense Medal. Bottom left to right - Vietnam Service Medal
with campaign star and Fleet Marine device, Vietnamese Campaign Star
with 1960 bar, Vietnamese Gallantry Cross with palm.

United States Ribbon Devices. Top left to right - Silver Star with small oak leaf cluster, Purple Heart with early style large oak leaf cluster, World War I Victory Medal with army service bars. Bottom left to right - Navy Good Conduct Medal with dated additional award bars, American Defense Service Medal with Base bar, American Campaign Medal.

CHAPTER IX

THE IRON CROSS OF PRUSSIA AND GERMANY

There are few collectors of Orders, Medals and Decorations who have not heard of, seen, or possessed an Iron Cross. With a history going back to 1813 it is one of the oldest valor decorations. It is also distinctive in its name. It is actually a cross made of iron.

Thus it was decided to single out this award, and go into more detail, and illustrate the detail.

Although it has been awarded for a number of conflicts since its founding 1813, it has not been awarded continuously. Originally founded in 1813 to reward valor in the War of Liberation with France, it was not awarded again until it was re-established with the date 1870 for the Franco-Prussian War of 1870-1871. The Iron Cross was subsequently re-established again in 1914, 1939, and then reissued in a denazified form (without the swastika) in 1957.

From 1813 to 1914 there were three classes. The Grand Cross, worn on a neck ribbon, rarely awarded, a first class pinback award, and a second class on a ribbon. In order to win the first class the second class had to have been awarded previously. In two cases, to Marshal Bluecher in 1813, and Field Marshal von Hindenburg in World War I, a breast star was awarded as a mark of very special favor. Such a star was struck for the 1939 issue, but never awarded.

In 1895, to commemorate the 25th anniversary of Germany's victory in the Franco-Prussian War a set of commemorative oakleaves was granted to be worn on the ribbon of the II Class Cross, see photo. In 1914 holders of the 1870 Iron Cross II Class, who qualified for the 1914 Iron Cross II Class received a bar to be worn over the ribbon. See photo.

In 1939 the Iron Cross evolved into a more complicated award. In addition to the I and II Classes there was a Grand Cross neck badge, awarded once only to Field Marshal Goering. Between the Grand Cross and the Iron Cross I Class there was established a neck decoration to be called the Knight's Cross of the Iron Cross. This cross was to be embellished with oakleaves; oakleaves and swords; oakleaves, swords, and diamonds; and finally, the Golden Knight's Cross with golden oakleaves and swords, with diamonds (awarded only once.)

In addition, to the holders of the Iron Cross II Class 1914 a bar was added for those who were entitled to the Iron Cross II Class 1939. Similarly, there was a bar for the Iron Cross I Class 1914, which was worn pinned on directly above the cross, or in some cases welded on to the top of the 1914 Cross I Class.

The Iron Cross I Class 1914 and to a lesser extent the 1939 issue, are much more complicated than would appear. According to the statutes of this award the official striking was to be a pin back piece. These pieces were also flat. When placed on a level surface they would lie flat.

However, as the manufacturing was done by private firms, as opposed to a government mint, there appeared many variations. The most common variation was a vaulted or arched piece. The arms of the cross do not lie flat. Instead when placed on a level surface they are raised. Apparently, recipients of these awards went to these private firms and had other types made, with a variety of fasteners.

Therefore, one can find Iron Crosses with hooks, screw backs, and nuts. Some of the photographs following this section show very clearly some of these different types, by showing the reverses as well.

It is possible to form an Iron Cross I Class collection. The extent of your collection may depend on your patience.

Some comments about hallmarks and fakes are in order. The 1914 Iron Cross II Class is usually marked with maker's initials on the ribbon ring. The I Class is often marked with initials, a maker's name, or silver content. I Class crosses which are not silver and iron, may have no hallmarks if produced in the 1920's, and perhaps hallmarked with a number or an L/number.

It is considered that any piece marked L/58 is a copy. I have been advised that a Knight's Cross of the Iron Cross marked L/12 should be view with suspicion. The Knight's Crosses were commonly marked on the suspension with a silver number, 800 or 900, and a manufacturer's number like 21. The oakleaves, the oakleaves and swords, and the oakleaves, swords and diamonds were marked separately on the reverse. See photographs.

There are some excellent references which go into great detail. Consult the bibliography for further reading.

The Prussian Iron Cross I Class. Top left and right- 1914 Screwback. Centre - 1870 vaulted pinback. Bottom left - 1914 vaulted screwback. Bottom right - 1914 vaulted pinback.

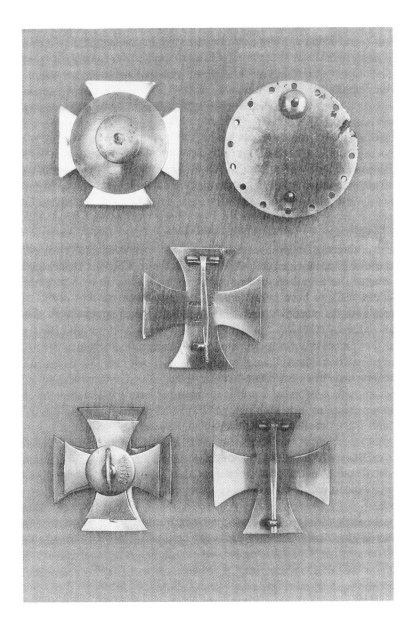

Reverse of the facing page showing pinback and screwback methods of attachment.

Top left - I Class 1914 with I Class bar 1939 attached. Bottom left - I Class 1914 with I Class bar 1939 unattached. Right - II Class 1914 with II class bar 1939.

The 1939 Knight's Cross of the Iron Cross with oakleaves and swords in issue case.

The 1914 "Hindenburg" Star.

GLOSSARY

The following terms are some that the collector is likely to come across while pursuing this hobby:

BADGE-refers usually to the part of an Order which hangs from a ribbon. It is most often enameled.

BAR or **CLASP**-refers to a device affixed to the medal, affixed to the ribbon, or slid over the ribbon, which will identify a campaign operation or commemorate some special activity in addition to that which is represented by the medal itself. In the case of some British items it is used to indicate a second or subsequent award.

"BLUE MAX" - nickname for the Prussian Pour Le Mérite Order.

BRONZE/GILT-refers to the practice of gold plating or coloring to enhance an item's appearance, or to indicate its class.

CASED-found in its original container, often made of wood with a leather or cloth covering. China and Japan also used lacquered cases for some of their awards.

CASTING-an item made from a mold rather than a die. Many copies are cast from an original. Through a magnifying glass the surface will appear pitted.

CIVIL-refers to an award which is awarded for non-combat operations. It may be given to both military and civil personnel depending on the regulations or statutes for the particular item.

CLAM SHELL-refers to the back plate of a screw back decoration like the Iron Cross I Class of Germany. The lines on the round plate are reminiscent of a clam's shell.

CLASS-this refers to the level of, the grade of, or the precedence of an award. Sometimes classes are listed by number with the first being the highest. In Spain the I Class is the lowest of an Order. Other times classes are listed by name, such as: GRAND CROSS-consisting of a badge worn on a sash, and a breast star, and sometimes a collar or chain. GRAND OFFICER-consisting of a neck badge, and a breast star, COMMANDER WITH STAR, COMMANDER I CLASS, or KNIGHT COMMANDER (Great Britain)-see Grand Officer. COMMANDER-a neck badge. OFFICER-a breast badge worn on a ribbon (may be called Knight I Class), and usually in gold, silver/gilt or bronze/gilt metal. KNIGHT-a breast badge worn on a ribbon in silver or silvered metal. While many Orders have five classes, there are some that have only one, some three, and some eight.

COLLAR or **CHAIN**-worn with the highest class of some Orders, or with one class Orders around the neck, with the badge of the Order hanging from it. They can be of gold, silver/gilt, bronze/gilt, with some enameling. Very sparingly awarded.

COURT MOUNTED-refers to a style of mounting where the ribbon is extended below the award, as well as above it, with some material to stiffen the ribbon behind it. A pin is attached for fastening on the recipient's garment. So called because it was specially favored for royal court or formal wear.

CRAVAT-term used in the U.S.A. to denote a neck ribbon for an Order, or for the Medal of Honor.

DENAZIFIED-refers to the awards of the III Reich which can be worn in Germany only in a form with the swastika removed. This does not apply to those of the Nazi Party and its various auxiliaries which may not be worn at all. Thus, all permitted items have been redesigned to eliminate the swastika. In the case of the Iron Cross oakleaves appear on the obverse centre.

DIE STRUCK-refers to an item struck from a die, rather than a casting from a mold. While there are die struck copies, originals are almost always die struck. The features will usually be clear and precise, whereas a casting is likely to be blurred and pitted.

EDGE KNOCK-this term is employed by the British collector to refer to a dent in the edge of the medal. A badly knocked medal will be avoided by the collector unless it is rare or very cheap.

FIXED SUSPENDER-the suspension on top of the medal through which the ribbon (ring) will go, does not turn.

FOULED ANCHOR- a rope is wrapped around the anchor-early issues of the U.S. Navy Medal of Honor.

GERMAN SILVER- not silver, but a nickel compound which has a silver appearance.

GILT-gold coloring or gold plating. Thus, the term gold/gilt should not be used.

GOLD(EN)-the use of this word does not always mean that the item concerned is made from the precious metal. It may be used to describe the appearance or class of the item, and be gilt on some other metal.

HALLMARK-a mark put on the item to indicate the manufacturer, and/or the metallic content. It may be a maker's initials, name, emblem, or a number, or a combination of these. See Jeffrey Jacob's COURT JEWELERS OF THE WORLD for further reference.

INSIGNIA-this term is used to indicate the various parts of an Order, such as badge, sash and breast star.

JUMP RING-the ring which goes through the suspension ring at the "top" of the award; the ribbon would normally go through this.

KD-abbreviation of Kriegs Dekoration-see below.

KLEINE DEKORATION-refers to the practice, mainly Austrian or Hungarian, of wearing an enameled device on the ribbon of a lower class of an Order or Decoration to denote the holding a higher award of that grade. For example the recipient of a I Class Military Merit Cross would wear the badge of a III Class with the Kleine Dekoration on it.

KRIEGS DEKORATION-an enameled wreath placed around Austrian or Hungarian award to denote war service, or service at the front.

LAPEL BAR or **LAPEL PIN**-in the U.S.A. refers to a small metal and enamel bar worn on the lapel of civilian clothes to indicate the award of some decoration.

MILITARY-when applied to an award indicates that it is either specifically a military one, or that it becomes a military award by the addition of a device like swords, or by the wearing of a special ribbon as in the case of the British Empire Order. The British Order of the Bath has two distinct sets of insignia for its military and civil classifications.

MINIATURE-a small replica of a Order, Medal or Decoration which is worn when the full size item is not. Some are of very high quality, and eagerly sought after by collectors. Especially favored are earlier pieces.

MOUNTED-refers to a group of items to the same recipient being attached by the ribbons to a pin bar for wearing. There are many ways of mounting, which vary by country.

NAMED-name of the recipient is engraved or impressed (stamped) on the rim or reverse of the award. Found most frequently on British campaign medals, and some British decorations.

NAME ERASED-refers to the name of the recipient being ground off the medal. The value of the item is reduced considerably.

NAMED CASE-the name of the award is stamped on the front or top cover of the case.

OAKLEAF-a small oakleaf spray worn on British medals to indicate a citation for gallantry, a "mention in despatches".

OAK LEAF CLUSTER-a small spray of bronze or silver oakleaves worn on the ribbon bar or the ribbon of U.S. Army or Air Force decorations to signify further awards. Corresponds to the British second award bars. The U.S. Navy uses a gold star instead.

OAK LEAVES-a spray of silver or golden oak leaves attached to an Order or an award as a mark of special distinction. This is primarily a German practice. In the case of the Knight's Cross of Iron Cross 1939, the oak leaves were used to create a higher grade of the award.

OBVERSE-the front of an Order, Medal, or Decoration.

PIN BACK-with awards not to be worn on a ribbon, a pin was attached on the reverse, with a catch, to fasten on to the uniform or other clothing.

PITTING-the characteristic of a cast piece, which under close examination will appear to have a large number of tiny holes. Pitting can also be caused by mounted medals striking each other. A case in point is the British Egypt Medal being struck by its companion Egyptian piece, the Khedive's Star.

PLANCHET-term used in the U.S.A. to refer to the main part of the medal, excluding its suspension.

POT METAL-in the two world wars shortages of metal because of the war effort resulted of what ever being available being "thrown in the pot" for the manufacture of awards. In Germany & Austria referred to as "kriegs Metal" or war metal. Thus one can see the Bavarian Military Merit Cross III Cl with swords and without crown in war metal, as well as several Austrian World War I awards.

PRECIOUS METAL CONTENT-many items may have been made from precious metals, such as gold and silver. An Austrian gold mark might be 750 indicating 18 karat gold. A Russian gold mark might be 56. Silver marks might be 800, 900, or even 925, 938, or even 958. American silver items are usually marked sterling. Some pieces appearing gold will be marked 1/20 10KGF, or one twentieth 10 karat gold filled.

PRINZEN- German term originally applied to the practice of awarding smaller size insignia, especially breast stars, to very young princes (prinzen) of royal houses.

RENAMED-the name of the original recipient has been removed and replaced by another. Usually, renamed medals have considerably less value, unless the renaming was officially done, as was the case with some British campaign medals.

RESTRIKE-the reissue of an item, either from original or newly made dies. This may indicate an unauthorized issue.

REVERSE-the back of an Order, Medal or Decoration.

RIBBON-the piece of material that an award hangs from. Originally silk, they may be of cotton, rayon or nylon.

RIBBON BAR-a narrow piece of ribbon mounted on a bar for wearing on a uniform in place of an original award.

RIBBON BAR DEVICES-small emblems worn on the ribbon bar to indicate some special distinction, such as combat service etc.

ROSETTE-refers to a circular piece of ribbon on a stiff backing which is place on the ribbon of an Order to indicate the IV Class or Officer, as in the case of the Legion of Honor. It can also be employed to indicate the higher grade of an award such as the Belgian Military Cross I Class. It is also employed in a miniature form to be worn in the buttonhole of, or on the lapel of a civilian coat. See also Lapel bar, lapel pin for the U.S.A.

SCREW BACK-refers to a screw like piece of metal fastened to the reverse of a decoration or award, which will then go through a hole in the tunic or coat, and has a nut or plate which fastens it securely. The plate may be hallmarked by the maker. Many of the awards of the Soviet Union were screw back items.

SILVER-the precious metal. Found in a variety of grades. In the U.S.A. marked sterling(.925) or 925 parts out of 1000. European silver hallmarks usually range from 800 to 900; but could be seen as 938, 958 or even 968.

The Imperial Russian silver hallmark was usually 84 (or 84 parts out of 96, and thus slightly below sterling standard of 925.)

SILVERED-a silver plated award.

STECKKREUZ-a German term referring to a pinback award-such as an Iron Cross I Class.

SUSPENSION-refers to the attachment at the top of the medal so that a ribbon can be worn with the item.

SWIVEL SUSPENSION-the suspension at the top of the medal turns, so that you can display either the obverse or reverse as you wish. Many British campaign medals swivel.

TINSEL STAR-A breast star made of metallic thread on a cloth backing. Frequently covered with sequins. In use till mid 19th century when replaced by metal stars. (See breast star.)

VAULTED-refers to the award having an arched appearance as opposed to lying flat. A clear example of this is the flat breast stars by Keibel and the vaulted breast stars of Eduard for the Order of St Stanislas of Imperial Russia.

WAR DECORATION-or Kriegs Dekoration-is a wreath which is placed on some Austro-Hungarian awards to indicate a military or wartime award.

WITH SWORDS-the addition of swords makes an award into a military or wartime one. The swords may be fastened between the arms of a cross., or fastened at the top, or on both at the same time. When swords are worn on the ring of an Order badge, the breast star will have them above the device, or badge centered on it.

WITHOUT SWORDS-an award without swords, for example the Bavarian Military Merit Order or Cross, will signify that it was given for a non-combat situation or to a non-military person.

BIBLIOGRAPHY

A bibliography on a subject of collector interest is of necessity a matter of opinion, rather than being composed solely of sources of information. I do not pretend that it covers every book on the subject. However, it does include my selection based on books in my own collection, as well as works suggested by other authors.

Where possible I have made comments pertinent to the work in question to help the collector choose. Nevertheless, the inclusion or exclusion of a reference from this bibliography is not to be taken as a statement as to the worth of said book.

Abbott, P. & Tamplin J. **BRITISH GALLANTRY AWARDS**-London 1982-Second Edition. A must book on the subject.

Angolia, J. **FOR FUHRER & FATHERLAND**-Volume I-The Military Awards of the III Reich; Volume II-The Political Awards of the III Reich-San Jose California-1976 & 1978.

Artuk, I. & Artuk, C. **THE OTTOMAN ORDERS**-Istanbul 1967-in Turkish & English.

Babin, L. **FOREIGN WAR MEDALS, ORDERS & DECORATIONS**-Rochester N.Y. c/ 1952.

Bascape, G. **THE ORDERS OF KNIGHTHOOD AND THE NOBILITY OF THE REPUBLIC OF SAN MARINO**-Delft, The Netherlands 1973.

Bax, W. **RIDDERORDEN, EERETEEKENEN, DRAAGTEEKENS EN PENNINGEN**- Maastrict, The Netherlands.

Belden, B. **UNITED STATES WAR MEDALS**-ANS NY 1916-reprinted by Norm Flayderman 1962.

Bell, C. **OFFICERS & MEN AT THE BATTLE OF MANILA BAY**-1972-a roll of recipients of the Manila Bay (Dewey) Medal.

Berghman, A. **NORDISKA ORDNER OCH DEKORATIONER**-Malmo, Sweden 1949.

Burke, Sir Bernard. **THE BOOK OF ORDERS OF KNIGHTHOOD AND DECORATIONS OF HONOUR**-London 1858.

Cardinale, H.E. **ORDERS OF KNIGHTHOOD, AWARDS, AND THE HOLY SEE**. Gerrards Cross, England 1983. The title is somewhat misleading, as it deals with Orders from several countries besides the Vatican State. It treats the subject from a religious viewpoint, which is apt since the whole matter in Europe stems from religious influence.

Castren, K. **LES ORDERS NATIONAUX DE LA FINLANDE**-Helsinki 1975.

Chalif, D. **MILITARY & AIRCREW BADGES OF THE WORLD**- Volume I- Albania to Hungary-San Jose, California 1982.

Cole, H. **CORONATION AND ROYAL COMMEMORATIVE MEDALS**-1877-1977- London 1977.

Davis, B. **BADGES & INSIGNIA OF THE THIRD REICH** 1933-1945-Poole, England 1983.

De la Bere, Sir Ivan. **THE QUEEN'S ORDERS OF CHIVALRY**-London 1961.

Delande, M. **DECORATIONS-FRANCE ET COLONIES**-Paris 1934. Especially useful to show variations of the Legion of Honor. Section on World War I items is spoiled by the fact that many pieces shown are copies.

de la Puente y Gomez, F. **CONDECORACIONES ESPANOLAS**-Madrid 1953.

Dimacopoulos, G. **GREEK ORDERS AND MEDALS**-Athens 1961-in Greek and English.

Dorling, T. **RIBBONS AND MEDALS**-revised by A. Purves, London 1983. Best comprehensive work available. Mainly British in content, but large foreign section including U.S.A.

Edkins, D. **THE PRUSSIAN ORDERN POUR LE MÉRITE**-The History of the Blue Max. Falls Church, Virginia 1981.

Elvin, C. **HANDBOOK OF THE ORDERS OF CHIVALRY**-London 1893.

Ercoli, E. **LE MEDAGILE, AL VALORE, AL MERITO E COMMEMORATIVO**-Military & Civil Awards of Sardinia & Italy (excluding Orders) 1793-1976-Milan 1976.

Feyver, W. editor **THE GEORGE MEDAL**-London 1980.

Forman, A. **FORMAN'S GUIDE TO THIRD REICH GERMAN AWARDS...AND THEIR VALUES**-1988-also gives values for documents and cases.

Gillingham, H. **ITALIAN ORDERS OF CHIVALRY AND MEDALS OF HONOR**- N.Y. 1922

...SPANISH ORDERS OF CHIVALRY AND MEDALS OF HONOR-N.Y. 1926.

Gordon, L. **BRITISH BATTLES AND MEDALS**-6th edition-extensively revised by E.C. Joslin, A. Litherland & B. Simpkin. The major work on British Campaign Medals, and a must book for collectors of this series.

Gritzner, M. **HANDBUCH DER RITTER UND VERDIENSTORDERN**-Leipzig 1893; reprinted Graz, Austria 1962-an early compendium of Orders of the World.

Hamelman, W. & Martin, D. **THE HISTORY OF THE PRUSSIAN POUR LE MÉRITE ORDER**-Volume I-1740-1812-Hamburg 1982.

Hamelman, W. **THE HISTORY OF THE PRUSSIAN POUR LE MÉRITE ORDER**-Volume II-1813-1888; Volume III 1888-1918-Dallas, Texas 1986.

Hazleton, A. **THE RUSSIAN IMPERIAL ORDERS**-N.Y. 1932.

Hieronymussen, P. **ORDERS, MEDALS & DECORATIONS OF BRITAIN & EUROPE**-London 1967. An extremely useful work on European awards after WWII. Hundreds of items in color, plus drawings. Originally published in Danish & German.

Ingraham, K. **HONORS, MEDALS AND AWARDS OF THE KOREAN WAR 1950-1953**-Binghamton NY 1993.

Jacob, J. **COURT JEWELERS OF THE WORLD**-Cherry Hill, N.J. 1978. Of the highest importance for collectors of Orders.

Jocelyn, A. **AWARDS OF HONOUR-THE ORDERS, DECORATIONS AND AWARDS OF GREAT BRITAIN AND COMMONWEALTH FROM EDWARD III TO ELIZABETH II**-London 1956.

Jorgensen, P. **DANISH ORDERS AND MEDALS**-Copenhagen 1964.

Joslin, E. **STANDARD CATALOGUE OF BRITISH ORDERS, DECORATIONS AND MEDALS**-London-several editions.

Kahl, R. **INSIGNIA, DECORATIONS AND BADGES OF THE THIRD REICH AND OCCUPIED COUNTRIES**-Kedichem, The Netherlands-c.1970.

Kerrigan, E. **AMERICAN WAR MEDALS AND DECORATIONS**-revised edition- 1990. A major work on U.S. awards.

Klenau, Arnhard Graf. **EUROPAISCHE ORDEN AB 1700-KATALOG OHNE DEUTSCHLAND**-1978.

Klietman, G. **DEUTSCHE AUSZEICHNEN**-Berlin 1971-an important work on German items from 1870-1945. It has a separate photo section.

...**PHALERISKTK RUMANIEN**-Berlin 1975. This book on Rumanian Orders etc is in English and German, and is profusely illustrated.

...**POUR LE MÉRITE UND TAPFERKEITSMEDAILLE**-Berlin 1966. A soft covered book of the highest utility. Covers Germany and her allies in both World Wars-with handy black & white photo section.

Kraft, H. **DEUTSCHE LUFTFAHRTABZEICHEN BIS 1945**-Hamburg 1983.

Laslo, A. **THE INTERALLIED VICTORY MEDALS OF WORLD WAR I**-1st & 2nd editions-1986 & 1992. A book which has made available to collectors of this series a serious and comprehensive work.

Littlejohn, D. & Dodkins, C. **ORDERS, DECORATIONS, MEDALS AND BADGES OF THE THIRD REICH**-Mountain View, California-Volume I (including Danzig) 1968: Volume II 1973.

Littlejohn, D. **FOREIGN LEGIONS OF THE THIRD REICH**-IV Volumes- San Jose, California-1979 etc. Useful for lesser known awards of the Nazi puppet groups.

Lippe, Prince Ernst August zur. ORDERN UND AUSZEICHNEN-Munich 1958.

McDowell, C. **MILITARY AND NAVAL AWARDS OF THE UNITED STATES**-Springfield, Virginia 1984. The best book on the subject now available. Well written and illustrated. Covers the decorations.

Mayo, J. **MEDALS AND DECORATIONS OF THE BRITISH ARMY AND NAVY**-2 volumes-London 1897.

MEDALS YEARBOOK-value guide to British awards-London 1983, in several editions.

NATIONAL GEOGRAPHIC-December 1919 and October 1943-includes color illustrations of all U.S. awards to date.

Nimmergut, J. **ORDEN EUROPAS**-Munich 1981.

...**ORDEN & EHRENZEICHEN VON 1800-1945**-Munich 1983-several editions-priced catalogue of German awards.

Orders and Medals Research Society of Great Britain. **JOURNAL**.

Orders and Medals Society of America. **THE MEDAL COLLECTOR**.

O'Toole, E. **DECORATIONS AND MEDALS OF THE REPUBLIC OF IRELAND**-London 1972.

Paris Mint. **DECORATIONS OFFICIELLES FRANCAISE**-Paris 1954-Published by the Paris Mint. Comprehensive and useful. Many color plates.

Peterson, J. **ORDERS AND MEDALS OF JAPAN AND ASSOCIATED STATES**-Chicago, 1967. Monograph No. 1 of the Orders and Medals Society of America. An excellent reference in English on this subject, with precise details on all Japanese awards.

Pownall, H. **KOREAN CAMPAIGN MEDALS 1950-1953**-pamphlet London c. 1954.

Prowse, A. **THE IRON CROSS OF PRUSSIA AND GERMANY**-New Zealand 1971-an extremely useful aid to this decoration.

214

Purves, A. COLLECTING MEDALS AND DECORATIONS-London 1983 (several editions). One of the must books for the collector of British awards.

...THE MEDALS, DECORATIONS AND ORDERS OF THE GREAT WAR 1914-1918. London 1975. The best book available on the subject in English. Many illustrations; pictures of U.S. and Japanese Victory Medals are of copies.

...THE MEDALS, DECORATIONS AND ORDERS OF WORLD WAR II 1939-1945. Similar in nature to the previous book, and extremely useful.

Quinot, H. ORDERS DE CHEVALERIE ET DECORATIONS BELGES DE 1830 A 1963. 1st Edition-Brussels, 1963.

Renault, J. LA LEGION D'HONNEUR-Paris, 1925. A massive and rare work which deals very thoroughly with subject. Also pictured are some early French awards.

Riley, D. UNCOMMON VALOR-Decorations, badges and service medals of the U.S. Navy and Marine Corps. USA 1980. A small, but handsome book showing all awards in color, with a general commentary for the reader.

Risk, J. BRITISH ORDERS AND DECORATIONS-N.Y. 1945. A useful discussion by a leading expert.

...HISTORY OF THE ORDER OF THE BATH-London, 1972. A thorough discussion of the subject.

Robles, P. U.S. MILITARY MEDALS AND RIBBONS-Rutland, Vermont 1971. Shows all U.S. military awards in color. Subject matter is general in nature.

Romanoff, Prince Dmitri. THE ORDERS, MEDALS AND HISTORY OF THE KINGDOM OF BULGARIA-Denmark 1982. An excellent presentation in English on an interesting country.

...THE ORDERS, MEDALS AND HISTORY OF GREECE-Denmark 1987-similar in nature to above.

...**THE ORDERS, MEDALS AND HISTORY OF MONTENEGRO**-II Edition- Denmark 1987-an interesting presentation in English on a country that no longer exists.

Roncetti, G. and Denby, E. **THE CANADIANS IN SOUTH AFRICA**-Toronto-an important reference regarding the Queen's South Africa Medal to Canadian recipients.

Rosignoli, G. **AIR FORCE BADGES AND INSIGNIA OF WORLD WAR II**-N.Y. 1977.

...**ARMY BADGES AND INSIGNIA OF WORLD WAR II**-Book I-Poole, England 1972; Book II 1975.

...**NAVAL AND MARINE BADGES AND INSIGNIA OF WORLD WAR II**-Poole, England 1980.

...**RIBBONS OF ORDERS, DECORATIONS AND MEDALS**-Poole, England 1976. Very useful for identifying many medals, although the colors are not always true. Discussion is very limited.

Schlaich de Bosse. **LES DISTINCTION HONORIFIQUES AU PAYS DE LUXEMBOURG 1430-1961**-Luxembourg, 1962.

Schreiber, G. **DIE BAYERISCHEN ORDEN UND EHRENZEICHEN**-Munich 1964.

Sculfort, V. **DECORATIONS, MEDAILLES, MONNAIES DU MUSEE DE L'ARMEE**-Paris 1912. French and foreign awards in the National Army Museum.

Smyth, Sir John. **THE STORY OF THE GEORGE CROSS**-London 1966.

...**THE STORY OF THE VICTORIA CROSS**-London 1963.

Strandberg, J. & Bender, R. **THE CALL OF DUTY**-San Jose, CA 1994. A superbly illustrated book, with some excellent and interesting material shown . Discussion is general in nature.

Tancred, G. **HISTORICAL RECORD OF MEDALS AND HONORARY DISTINCTIONS**-London 1891.

U.S. Senate Committee on Labor and Public Welfare. **MEDAL OF HONOR 1863-1968**-Washington D.C. 1968. Official U.S. Government publication on this decoration; with list of recipients, citations as well as pertinent information.

Vernon, S. **VERNON'S COLLECTORS' GUIDE TO ORDERS, MEDALS AND DECORATIONS (with valuations)**. Baldwin, NY 1986, 1st edition; Wildomar, CA 1990, 2nd edition; Temecula CA 1995, 3rd edition.

...**SALES CATALOGUES** 1967-1995

Vietnam Council on Foreign Relations. **AWARDS AND DECORATIONS OF VIETNAM**-1972. All the awards of South Vietnam, civil and military, with explanation in English and Vietnamese.

von Hessenthal, W. and Schreiber, G. **DIE EHRENZEICHEN DES DEUTSCHEN REICHES**-Berlin 1940. The major work on the medals and decorations of Germany and States up to 1940, and Austria (then part of Germany), and a must book for the collector of German awards. Does not deal with Orders. Extremely rare. It has been reprinted.

von Heyden, H. **EHRENZEICHEN IN FRANKREICH UND BELGIEN**-Frankfurt am Main 1903.

von Prochazka, R. **OSTERREISCHISCHES OFDENS HANDBUCH**-3 volumes 1979-covers Austrian awards to date. Very comprehensive, with many clear illustrations.

WALDORF ASTORIA ALBUM-colored picture album of German Orders & Decorations. c.1930; 280 items shown.

Weaver, B., Gleim, A. and Farek, D. **THE WEST INDIES NAVAL CAMPAIGN OF 1898. THE SAMPSON MEDAL, THE SHIPS AND THE MEN.** - Arlington, Virginia 1986. An important book for the U.S. medal collector, which illustrates in complete detail the fascinating story of the "Sampson Medal". A must reference to verify and identify this series.

Werlich, R. **ORDERS AND DECORATIONS OF ALL NATIONS**-Military & Civil. II Edition-Washington D.C. 1964. An encyclopedia on the subject. Very useful on U.S. civilian awards. Shows only the highest class of Orders.

...RUSSIAN ORDERS, DECORATIONS AND MEDALS-Including Imperial Russia, Provisional Government, Civil War and the U.S.S.R.-II Edition Washington D.C. 1981. An important work for the collector-heavily illustrated. Does not show suspensions of medals.

Wrede, E. **FINLANDS UTMARKELSETECKEN**-Helsinki 1946. In Swedish, heavily illustrated.

Wyllie, R. **ORDERS, DECORATIONS AND INSIGNIA**-N.Y. 1927. U.S. and foreign awards.

INDEX OF COUNTRIES AND TOPICS

COLLECTORS' ORGANIZATIONS

Below are the names and addresses of some Collectors' organizations as of the writing of this book.

BUND DEUTSCHER ORDENSAMMLER e.v. Postfach 1260 Eisenbergstr 10, D-6497 Steinau a.d.Str. Germany
MEDAL SOCIETY OF IRELAND-c/o Michael A. Kavanagh, Secretary, Market Sq, Bunclody Co Wexford, Ireland.
MEDEC c/o Hugo Jacobs, President, Paasbloemstraat 81, 2060 Merksem, Belgium.
MILITARY COLLECTORS' CLUB OF CANADA-c/o Geoff Fairless, Secy/Treasurer, 15 Abel Pl., St Albert, Alta T8N 2Z5, Canada.
ORDENSHISTORISK SELSKAB-c/o Peter Ohm-Hieronymussen, President, Falkoneralle 79, DK 2000, Frederiksberg, Denmark.
ORDERS AND MEDALS RESEARCH SOCIETY-c/o Graham Grist, Librarian, 1, Roseberry Court Chesington, Surrey KT9 2DL, United Kingdom.
ORDERS AND MEDALS SOCIETY OF AMERICA-c/o J. Lelle, Secretary, Box 484, Glassboro NJ 08028.

Notes

Notes

Notes

Notes